TASTE

THE SECRETS of wine and FOOD APPRECIATION

PABLO ANTINAO

Copyright 2017 Pablo Antinao
First Publication 2017
Publisher: Park Place Publications
Phone: 831-649-6640
Mail: publishingbiz@sbcglobal.net
Web: www.parkplacepublications.com

ISBN: 978-1-943887-38-5

AUTHOR: Pablo Antinao
GRAPHIC DESIGN: Amparo Phillips

NO PART OF THIS PUBLICATION MAY BE REPRODUCED OR TRANSMITTED IN ANY FORM OR BY ANY MEANS, ELECTRONIC OR MECHANICAL, INCLUDING PHOTOCOPY, RECORDING OR ANY INFORMATION STORAGE AND RETRIEVAL SYSTEM, WITHOUT PERMISSION IN WRITING FROM THE COPYRIGHT OWNER(S)

TASTE

THE SECRETS of wine and FOOD APPRECIATION

PABLO ANTINAO

For my son, **Dimitri**, who brought to my life a different experience of love I can't express with words, and brought my inspiration for this book.

Why TASTE?

Throughout the duration of my ongoing career in the wine industry, I have been asked countless questions regarding wine; however, one of the most common questions is how to taste wine. The creation of TASTE has origins in a desire to bring more understanding and clarity to consumers regarding wine production, food pairing, and the fundamental importance of using the senses. I believe wine cannot be analyzed simply as a beverage. No, wine is connected with many elements, whether something as simple as enjoyment in our daily lives, or something as deep as our human history. It has been an active protagonist since the arrival of the Pilgrims and Christopher Columbus to the Americas. Wine is still in contemporary times a welcome guest in the lives and tables of an increasing number of people around the world.

Wine is a seductive beverage and because of this element of seduction, it cannot be seen simply as just another beverage. The seduction I refer to is related to the intimate and fundamental relationship human beings have with food and beverage, whether it is wine or beer, coffee or tea, spirits or liquors, or food itself. In my opinion, eating and drinking are one of the most important ways we pleasure our senses and nurture our souls.

Wine, like food, is connected with agriculture, biology, chemistry, history, philosophy and sociology. Wine involves art, laws and regulations, mystery and romance. The world of wine and food is a fascinating and captivating world.

My proposal and invitation to you is to educate yourself about the intimacy of wine and food, as well as learning more about the complex process that transforms mere grapes into your favorite wine. The answers not only rely on an intellectual explanation and understanding of the matter, but also require a deep exploration within yourself, so that you really connect with your senses. When that happens, you'll be ready to face and explore the world of wine and food with an open, yet critical, mind and with an amazing ability to TASTE the world around you!

Table of contents

01
Time: Growing Grapes and Making Seductive Wine

02
Awareness of the Senses

03
Some Descriptions of Classic World Varieties

04
Tools for Serving and Enjoying Wine

05
Enhancing Our Appreciation of Wine and Food

Wine

Wine, you are result of nature.
Wine, your father is the sun and the moon is your mother.
Like a child you start maturing with the veraison and become introverted and deep in the fall.
Wine, your roots are deep in the soil and like arms, your roots hug the dirt and kiss the water.

Wine, you are part of ceremonies, rituals, memories and events that have been part of every human journey.
Wine, you are and have been a passive protagonist and spectator in life and on tables in many homes.
We should never forget the ones who make history with their hard labor of love ... the stewards of the land.

Wine, you bring alive the senses.
Every time I sip and sniff you, you evoke memories.
Like a good kiss you can become memorable ... unforgettable.

Wine, time will shape your evolution with seductive flavors and sensual textures.
Wine, with patience you'll become a rainbow of beautiful colors and a fountain of pure pleasure.

Wine, you were made with Divine fruit.
Here in the north and there in the south, we sing the song of harvest during different times of the year and the beautiful melodies of the seasons allow us to remember how lucky we are.

Pablo Antinao

06

Where it all began

According to experts, grape cultivation began approximately 9,000 years ago, probably between the Black and Caspian seas. Eventually, Greek and Roman empires influenced the expansion of grape cultivation, which quickly spread throughout Europe. Later, various European colonists, merchants, and missionaries carried Vitis vinifera to Africa, Asia, and South and North America. European wine grapes were brought to the Americas by the Spanish conquistadors in the early 1500s, who intended to use them for sacramental purposes. Viticulture came to California with the Franciscan friars who built twenty-one missions, the first being San Diego de Alcala in 1769 and the last, San Francisco Solano, in Sonoma in 1823. The padres cultivated and grew mission grapes to use in Mass.

Meanwhile back East, cultivation of European vines was influenced by the arrival of Pilgrims in the New England colonies around 1620. The Pilgrims encountered new species, different from the traditional European Vitis vinifera. For example, Vitis lambrusca, Vitis berlandieri, and Vitis rupestris were discovered in the New World. Many of you are already familiar with Vitis lambrusca if you have eaten a peanut butter and jelly sandwich, as this is the grape variety used to make Concord jelly. Besides Concord grapes from Vitis lambrusca, Norton and Muscadine are other wine grape varieties native to North America that Pilgrims encountered. These are still grown today in eastern regions of the U.S.

It turns out the Pilgrims were not successful in the traditional, Old World style of winemaking due to poor climatic conditions and differences within the species of grapes. It wasn't until the arrival of the Huguenots from France during the seventeenth century that it became possible to make the nectar of Bacchus the Old World way. However, this hope quickly faded due to unsuitable climatic conditions for cultivating the traditional Vitis vinifera. It wasn't until the twenty-first century that winemaking in the eastern states finally took off due to an evolution in knowledge and research, as well as technological advances in the wine industry. Though all fifty states in the U.S. are making wine today, eastern states such as Virginia, New York and Michigan are making excellent wines and becoming well known regions in the wine world. A surprising fact given the complicated wine history this region holds.

01

Time for Growing Grapes and Producing Seductive Wine

Vitis vinifera

Over 10,000 varieties of Vitis vinifera are found world-wide and more than 1,300 are well known/commercial varieties. But don't worry, you don't have to memorize them all!

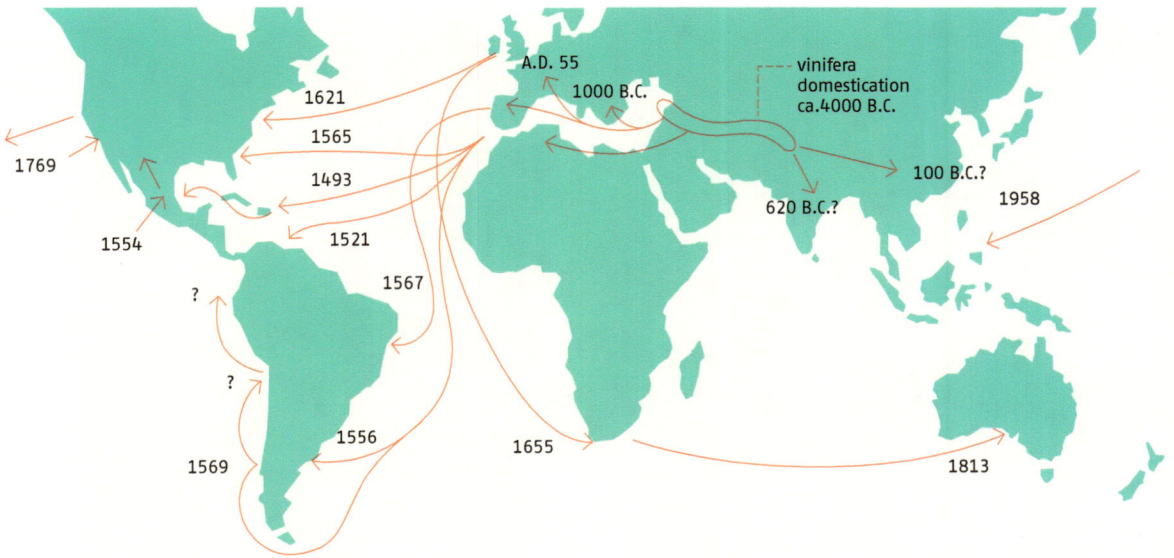

The spread of vitis vinifera in the world

World distribution of wine grape production

The Vine Cycle

Everything Started in the Vineyard

Today, there is an increasing amount of awareness when it comes to agricultural practices. Specifically, consumers are more conscious about their health, the environment, and how food affects their life, community and region. For example, I notice an increase in the number of farmers markets. More and more markets and restaurants are working with local growers, and even close friends are starting their own vegetable gardens. In my opinion, these organic and biodynamic movements prove not only that produce has better flavor when grown organically, but also demonstrate the growing interest in deeper core values, such as understanding/respecting nature and those who work with it.

With respect to wine, consumers are becoming more aware of the connection between grape growing and agriculture and they are starting to recognize that grapes are an agricultural product, just as carrots and tomatoes are. Location (climate, soil), production (conventional, biodynamic, organic), and how natural or manipulated the winemaking process are questions consumers should make when purchasing wine. These elements will affect the quality of the end product and should be taken into consideration.

In my interactions with people in restaurants, retail or tasting room settings, I am often asked, **"What is the best way to understand wine?"** My response is to encourage consumers to be open-minded and sample broad varieties and styles of wine, to connect with the senses, and educate themselves about how wine is produced. If people understand what is involved in the process, they will know what it takes to make a truly seductive wine.

14

Lets learn in general how wine is produced

As I said before, wine is an agricultural product. That said, in order to understand wine our approach needs to have an inclusive, holistic view. This way, we can understand how nature affects key elements like soil and climate that later determine many aspects of wine: tannins, sugar, acidity, and the overall balance of the desired wine.

Soil is a key element when describing how wines are produced. First of all, soil is going to be a major factor in water absorption, very important for the survival of the vineyard as well as the main source of nutrients for the vine. Without the proper soil and climate, it will be very difficult to grow quality grapes.

In California, the vine cycle begins around April when new shoots emerge from a dormant bud. The shoots typically grow during the months of April and May in coastal and cooler non-coastal areas. However, in the warmer Central Valley, the process starts earlier due to different climatic conditions. Vine flowers develop around the middle of May in general. This also varies depending on the region of California.

From there, baby grapes begin to grow but remain green, hard, and very acidic until about the middle or end of July. During veraison, the ripening of the grapes begins. Grapes start losing their acidity and as this happens, more sugar is naturally produced. Once grapes reach the optimum level of maturity, which is typically decided by the viticulturist and/or winemaker, the fruit is usually harvested around September or October. Again, this date varies depending on the variety, location and the weather conditions of that particular year. Harvest also depends on the style of wine, fruitier or drier, the winery wants to make.

In November or December, the vine loses its leaves and like a bear in winter, enters dormancy. Pruning in California usually takes place between the months of December and February. This is a fundamental process because it will determine next year's crop.

So now let us examine some aspects of grape growing more specifically

Grape Structure: The pigment (color) of grape berries that produces the color of red wine is found in the skin of the grape as well as some tannin. Most of the tannins are derived from the seeds and stalks. These contribute a bitter and astringent flavor to the wine and a tactile sensation on the palate. The pulp contains water, sugar, acids and flavor compounds. Finally, the bloom contains yeast and bacteria. As you can see, the grape contains many of the main elements that will play a key role in the winemaking process.

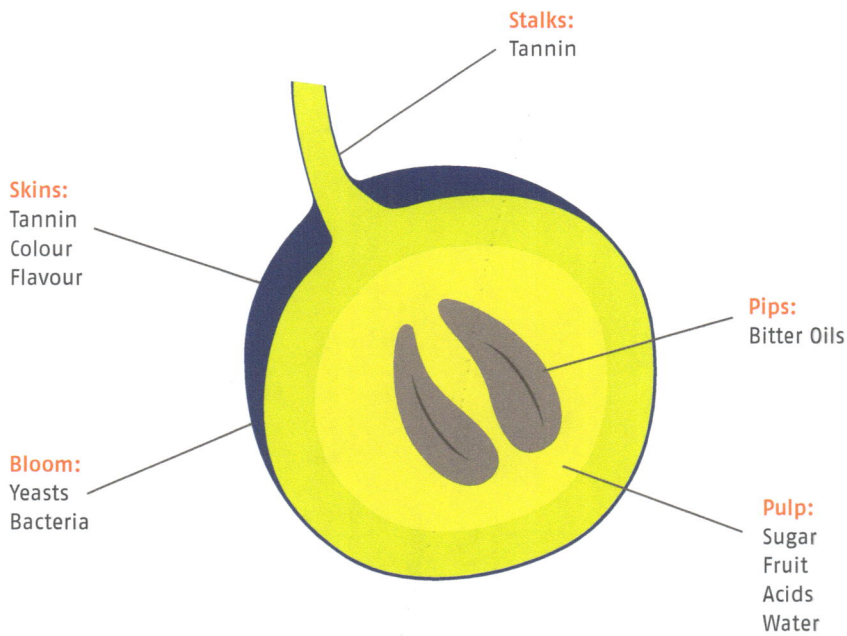

Stalks: Tannin

Skins: Tannin, Colour, Flavour

Bloom: Yeasts, Bacteria

Pips: Bitter Oils

Pulp: Sugar, Fruit, Acids, Water

Harvesting

This is probably one of the most fundamentally important decisions made by the winemaker. The decision to harvest wine grapes is key and theoretically is made on the basis of sugar and acid concentrations and appropriate pH. In the U.S., the measurement for sugar content in the grapes is known as the "Brix." The sugar must be high enough to produce the desired alcohol concentration, while the acidity must also be high enough to maintain the desired tartness and vibrant liveliness of the wine.

Varietal characteristics such as flavor, acidity, sweetness, color, texture and aromas are very important determinants for harvesting. These key varietal characteristics sometimes do not reach their optimal concentration levels at the same time. So, it is a normal practice of winemakers and/or viticulturists to carefully monitor the development of fruit as it nears maturity before harvest. They do this by tasting (eating) the fruit right off the vine! As you can see, nature is key and can provide optimal conditions to help the winemaker create a great wine. Without nature's fundamental role, it would be very challenging for the winemaker to produce an outstanding wine. Below you can see the evolution of grapes and their subsequent flavor characteristics.

General Berry Ripening Chart: Flavors and Aromas

BERRY CHARACTERISTICS	FLAVORS AND AROMAS	DESCRIPTION
Unripe Berries	Vegetal, Herbaceous	Grass Hay, Green, Bitter, Acidic, Tart, Sour
Optimal Maturity	Red and Black Fruits	Sweet, Juicy, Fresh, Optimal acidity, Soft tannins, variety of aromatic nuances
Overripe Berries	Jam and Bake Fruits	Overly sweet, Dry, Non-acidic, Mono-aromatic

Achieving the right level of ripeness when harvesting is key to making a great, seductive wine. The decision of when to harvest should be made based on the optimal level of maturity of the berries (grapes), which includes physiological ripeness of the berry (skin and pulp) and phenolic ripeness of the berry (seeds). This is a major balancing act provided by nature. That's why vintage of wine in certain years is important. Accomplishing this balance in the vineyard is not easy, because we depend on nature. "Man" can participate in this process, making adjustments to what nature failed to provide the berry. The mission of the winemaker is to strive to find the desired balance. Harvesting grapes after the window for optimal maturity passes means the grapes will have the characteristics of overripe berries (see Berry Ripening Chart above) and will need a great deal of cellar manipulation in order to achieve balance.

Pruning

A common, very important post-harvest practice is pruning. Pruning determines the yield (fruit) for next year's harvest and is a decision based on many factors. The winery will determine the pruning technique used based on economics, climatic zone/location, type of wine, and the philosophy of the winery. Wineries have choices in pruning styles to better suit their financial goals or to meet expectations about the quality of their wines. In other words, it is a matter of quality and quantity.

The most common styles of pruning are cane and spur. Cane pruning, the more challenging of the two, involves selecting one or two shoots from the previous season's growth and cutting them back between six to fifteen buds. These buds will form the basis of growth in the following year. In spur pruning, shoots are cut, leaving two or three buds, which will form the basis of growth in the following year. Spur pruning is much easier than cane pruning and oftentimes can partially be accomplished with machinery. The amount of buds that remain in the vineyard will determine the amount of yield. More buds mean more yield, less buds, less yield. In general, the higher the yield, the lower the quality.

Dormancy

Like all great cycles on Earth, wine production follows a cyclical nature. After harvest, vines will enter into a dormant state in winter. This dormant period leads to spring, where the vine cycle begins all over again. Alongside pruning, environmental conditions (dry or wet weather) and farming practices all influence quality and quantity next year's crop.

Dealing with Nature

All of us can agree that nature is beautiful. Living in California, I certainly appreciate nature every time I see the Pacific Ocean and the mountains. I have to say that California reminds me a lot of my homeland.

In addition to being breathtaking, nature is temperamental and unforgiving. In today's times human beings are responsible for the destruction of our environment in conjunction with bad policies and bad science, as Jane Jacobs points out in her book Dark Age Ahead. Today, my friends, we are living in the Anthropocene Era, during which Earth's physical changes are mainly driven by human activity. Whether the discussion is about climate, biodiversity, biochemistry or agriculture, we are negatively affecting our environment at an unprecedented rate, which in turn affects all of us. We see these impacts in the form of more frequent and destructive earthquakes, droughts, hurricanes, tornados and tsunamis. Unfortunately Chile and many other parts of the world experience nature's temperamental side very often. Nature has a way of making us remember how fragile and humble we are, whether it is through destruction or awe and beauty. How easily we forget our connectivity with nature. An important step in contributing to turning around this global crisis is to become mindful of the nourishment that nature provides for us. Climate change is real. Now let's take a more in-depth look at how climate affects the world of wine.

Favorable Climatic Conditions for Growing Grapes

Climate is so important for grape growing as it is for many different types of crops. In the case of grapes, a mild summer will usually ensure that the grapes ripen slowly. This leads to a balance in components such as acidity, tannins, sugars, and fruit structure. The balance of these elements is key to producing a seductive wine.

A dry, sunny summer and fall is essential for ripening grapes and avoiding rot and mildew. Any extreme temperatures will harm the grapes.

Climate must suit the viticultural needs of each specific grape variety. For example, Pinot Noir, Chardonnay, Riesling, and Pinot Gris all require a cooler climate. Zinfandel, Petit Syrah, and Granache require a warmer climate. Global warming is having an impact on viticulture and it will be interesting to see the effects on traditional regions as well the development of new regions. It won't be surprising if colder countries like Scotland or Ireland begin making wines due to their warmer temperatures caused by global warming.

Unfavorable Climatic Conditions

Extreme climatic conditions are not the best for growing grapes. Additionally, major climatic changes like frost, hail and strong winds can denude vines, which sounds interesting and sexy, but it is not good for vines. Denuding is particularly dangerous when the vine is flowering or the grapes are ripening and at their most vulnerable stage. Everybody feels vulnerable when naked, right? Well, at least personally I feel that way!

Heavy rain and/or cold temperatures during the flowering may cause imperfect fertilization, which results in a physiological grape disorder called millerandage (sounds complicated!). In simple words, this means the affected grapes contain no seeds, remain small, and are only partially developed, while the rest of the cluster is fully matured.

Persistent rain at or immediately before harvest can lead to diseases like rot or powdery mildew. This also dilutes the flavor compounds of the grapes. Both unfavorable conditions can be damaging to the development of healthy grapes, which eventually can lead to vinification (fermentation) problems.

On the other hand, if excessively high temperatures occur during harvest, this rapidly decreases the grape's acid level, making the grapes almost like raisins if they are harvested too late. This also creates problems during fermentation, which is explained later in the book. It is especially difficult to harvest grapes at an acceptable temperature in very hot areas, such as California's San Joaquin Valley and parts of Paso Robles, to name a few. As a result, some wineries harvest the grapes at night when they are at their coolest temperature. Again, we should expect that global warming is going to cause some interesting changes in the wine world ... unfortunately most changes are negative. It is my hope the changes do not affect the wine regions of the world too much.

Examples of Cool Regions

Burgundy and Alsace (France). Sonoma Coast, Russian River, Santa Lucia Highlands, Santa Maria and Santa Rita Hills (California). Casa Blanca and Bio-Bio (Chile). Marlborough (New Zealand), Tasmania in Australia.

Examples of Warm Regions

Lodi, the Sierra Foothills, San Joaquin Valley, Madera and Paso Robles (California). La Mancha (Spain), the Mendoza province of Argentina.

The Importance of Soil

Certainly climate is very important as we can see, but soil is equally important and many winemakers believe that soil can be even more important than climate.

Whether they are right or not, both are extremely important in growing quality grapes and perhaps any agricultural crop.

Soils affect the physiology of the vine through the ability to absorb and drain away water and through its heat-retention properties. Another fundamental aspect of soil is the contribution of nutrients, minerals and food it provides to the vines.

You've probably heard the word Terroir in a tasting room or at a winery. It sounds fancy and is commonly used among winemakers and wine associates in tasting rooms. So, what is Terroir? Generally speaking, Terroir is a term used to describe the soil's influence on the wine. Let's take a deeper look at Terroir and what the term really means.

Terroir has its origin in France and is a philosophically intrinsic way the French view soil beyond just simple soil. It refers to a set of special characteristics that are shared: geography, geology, people and climate.

Terroir ultimately gives an identity to the wine. Benedictine and Cistercian monks actually tasted the soil in their search for the perfect Terroir for Pinot Noirs. As comical and extreme as this may seem, some winemakers/viticulturists today still partake in tasting the soil to assess its Terroir. This French philosophical approach resonates with many wineries and winemakers around the world.

The Yin and Yang of Agriculture

Grapes are a delicious fruit and because of grapes, today we can enjoy delicious wine. However, like most agricultural crops, pests and disease threaten them. Grape vines are no exception. Some of these pests and diseases played an important part in the history of wine. Let me introduce to you one of the most destructive pests in the history of winemaking ... Ms. Phylloxera vastatrix.

Why is Ms. Phylloxera Vastatrix so important in the history of wine?

Phylloxera vastatrix (though I think "Devastatrix" should be the correct name for it) is the scientific name for the pest that devastated European vineyards in the late 19th century. *Phylloxera* still infests the soils of nearly all the world's winegrowing regions, with some exemptions such as Chile. (Well, I have to mention Chile since I was born down there ... so you can realize even more how unique the Chileans are.) At the time, it was considered the greatest disaster in the history of wine. If *Phylloxera* did not exist, who knows how the world of wine would be shaped today? Maybe California and French wines would be more affordable than they are ... who really knows?

As *Phylloxera* spread, it became apparent that something needed to be done to save Bacchus's nectar. After many years of obscure and exhaustive research to find the cure, finally one was found in grafting, which became the best solution to attack Ms. P*hylloxera*. The cure was discovered in the U.S. by Charles Valentine Riley in collaboration with his French colleague, Jules-Emile Planchon. Finally there became a solution through union, but not a union between Planchon and Riley ... these men created a union between a rootstock from a wild American species (*Vitis Lambrusca vitis rupestris*, and *Vitis riperia*) with a scion coming from a European *Vitis vinifera*.

The U.S.'s Contribution in the Battle against Phylloxera

Hundreds of rootstock varieties have been developed from various vine species. Guess what? Most of them are native to the U.S.! The most common rootstock varieties are *Vitis berlandieri*, *V. riparia*, and *V. rupestris*, because they are the most resistant to *Phylloxera*. The precise choice of rootstock is dependent on its suitability to the vine rootstock on which it is to be grafted (*Vitis vinifera* scion), as well as on its adaptability to the geographical location and soil type. The choice is very important because it can increase or decrease a vine's productivity, and thus has a strong effect on the quality of the wine produced from the grapes. In general, the lower the quantity of fruit, the higher the quality (under normal and healthy conditions of the vine).

Scion and rootstock divide)

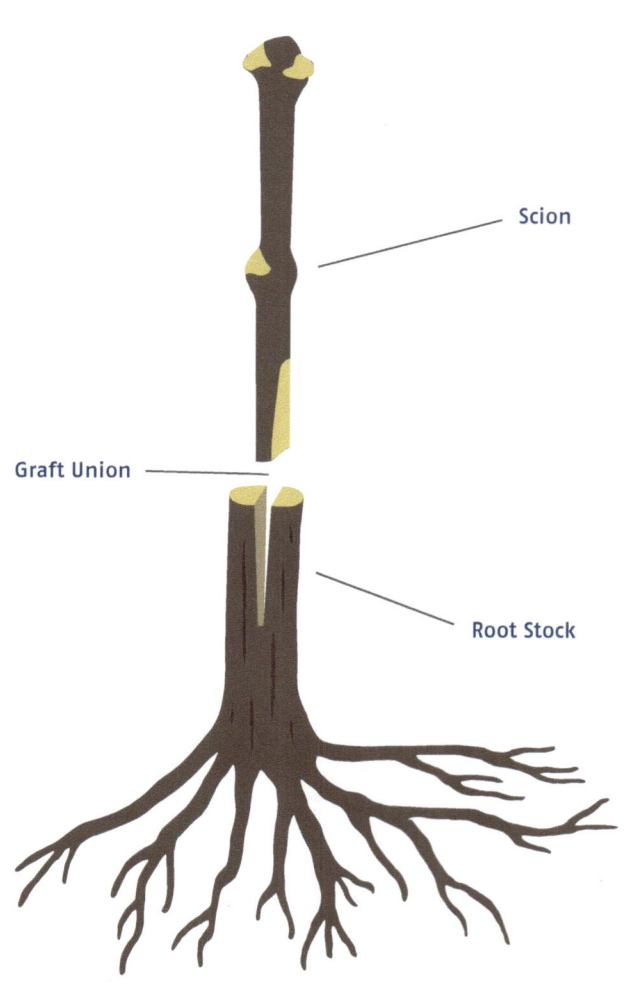

Phylloxera's Impact on the Wine Industry

Due to the great devastation *Phylloxera* had on various vineyards throughout Europe, to prevent any potential fraud and to ensure quality, the French government created the *Appellation d'Origene Controlee* (AOC). The AOC is a set of regulations that define regions and sub-regions of the wine country in France, as well as the quality of wine. The AOC is supervised by the the *Institut National de l'Origine et de la Qualité* (previously *Institut National des Appellations d'Origine*, INAO). France led the way in terms of developing the AOC system and soon enough, many countries in Europe and the New World were adopting similar regulations, with some country's regulations more flexible than others.

Here in the United States, the counterpart of the French AOC is the American Viticultural Areas system (AVA).

What is the AVA System in the U.S.?

Basically, it is our simplified version of the French AOC system. The function is to determine the geographical boundaries of the American Viticultural Areas (AVA). In other words, those are the areas where the grapes to produce wine are growing. The U.S. Treasury Department's Tobacco Tax and Trade Bureau (TTB) administers the AVAs. The TTB is in charge of collecting taxes on production and sales of alcohol and tobacco. It also sets Federal policies for wine label certification, varietal type alcohol content of the wine in the country where it was produced, and much more. Surprisingly, the AVA does not force a winery to reveal how the wine was made. Every winery chooses to share (or not) that information voluntarily with the public. Here we can see what the winery has to put on the label according the TTB.

Pablo's Winery

VINTAGE DATE

A vintage date on the label indicates the year in which the grapes were harvested. If a vintage date is shown on the label at all, an appellation of origin smaller than a country must also be shown. If an American or imported wine uses a State or county, or the foreign equivalent, as an appellation of origin, 85 percent of the grapes must be from that year; if a viticultural area or the foreign equivalent is used, the percentage is raised to 95 percent.

ESTATE BOTTLED

"Estate Bottled" means that 100 percent of the wine came from grapes grown on land owned or controlled by the winery, which must be located in a viticultural area. The winery must crush and ferment the grapes and finish, age, and bottle the wine in a continuous process on their premises. The winery and the vineyard must be in the same viticultural area.

APPELLATION OF ORIGIN

Appellation of origin is another name for the place in which the dominant grapes used in the wine were grown. It can be the name of a country, state, county or geographic region called a viticultural area, or their foreign equivalents.

A country, state, or county appellation or their foreign equivalent on the label means that at least seventy-five percent of the wine is produced from grapes grown in the place named.

VITICULTURAL AREA

An American viticultural area is a defined grape-growing region in the U.S. with geographic features, (such as soil and climate) that set it apart from the surrounding areas.

A viticultural area appellation on the label indicates that eighty-five percent or more of the wine was produced from grapes grown in the named area.

ALCOHOL CONTENT

A statement of alcohol content in percent by volume appears on most labels. As an alternative, some bottlers may label wine with an alcohol content from seven to fourteen percent as "Table Wine" or "Light Wine."

DECLARATION OF SULFITES

Required on any wine intended for interstate commerce that contains ten or more parts per million of sulfur dioxide. Not required for wines only sold in intrastate commerce.

BRAND NAME

The brand name is used to identify and market a wine. A brand name may not mislead the consumer about the age, identity, origin, or other characteristics of the wine.

VARIETAL DESIGNATIONS

Varietal designations are the names of the dominant grapes used in the wine. Cabernet Sauvignon, Chardonnay, Zinfandel, and Merlot are examples of grape varieties. A varietal designation on the label requires an appellation of origin and means that at least seventy-five percent of the grapes used to make the wine are of that variety, and that the entire seventy-five percent were grown in the labeled appellation (except "Vitis labrusca" grapes, such as Concord, which require at least fifty-one percent).

HEALTH WARNING STATEMENT

By law, this statement is required on all alcohol beverages containing one-half of a percent or more alcohol by volume.

OTHER DESIGNATIONS

Wine labels are not required to bear a varietal designation. Other designations may be used to identify the wine, such as Red Wine, Rose Wine, White Wine, Table Wine (if no more than 14% alcohol by volume) or Dessert Wine (if over 14% alcohol by volume).

Some imported wines are designated with a distinctive name which is permissible only on specific wines from a particular place or region within the country of origin, for example, Asti Spumanti from Italy and Bordeaux from France.

COUNTRY OF ORIGIN

Pursuant to regulations issued by U.S. Customs and Border Protection, a Country of Origin statement is required on containers of imported wines. Acceptable statements include "Product of, (insert name of country)" or "Produced in, (insert name of country)."

NAME AND ADDRESS

The name and address of the bottler or importer must appear on the container. It is also permissible for a bottler/importer to use a duly authorized trade name in place of its usual operating name.

Domestic wines may have this statement further qualified with terms such as "Produced," meaning that not less than seventy-five percent of the wine was fermented at the stated address, or "Vinted," which means that the wine was subjected to cellar treatment at the stated address.

NET CONTENTS 13

The net contents of a wine container must be stated in metric units of measure. Wine must be bottled in 50 ml, 100 ml, 187 ml, 375 ml, 500 ml, 750 ml, 1 L, 1.5 L, or 3 L sizes. Containers over 3 L must be bottled in quantities of even liters. No other sizes may be bottled.

Now lets take a look at some of the most widely used viticultural approaches.

As I mentioned before, wine starts in the vineyard. Quality of the grapes is fundamental in order for the winemaker to have a greater chance of making a memorable, seductive, great wine. Now you know that wine is a sub-product of agriculture, so it is very important to know how your favorite wine was created and how the grapes were grown. As customers in farmers markets begin identifying their favorite farmers for the quality and ethical/sustainable growing conditions of their fruits and vegetables, it is equally important to identify how wineries grow their grapes and make your favorite wine.

Conventional Viticultural Approaches

In conventional agriculture, chemical fertilizers are used to promote larger yields and protect against disease. These same chemicals are absorbed through the roots into the vine's sap and are then passed through leaves and stems into the fruit. Conventional 'chemical based' farming has a significant negative impact on soil, water quality/contamination, and the environment in general. Growers who farm with chemicals have to wear Hazmat suits and a breathing apparatus to protect them while spraying crops.

Organic Viticultural Approaches

Wines labeled "organic" and bearing the USDA organic seal must be made from organically grown grapes; that is, grapes grown in accordance with principles of organic farming. These typically exclude the use of artificial chemical fertilizers, pesticides, fungicides, herbicides and the organic use of yeast. Additionally, a wine in this category cannot have any added sulfites, and must give information to consumers identifying the agency that certified the wine as organic. Regarding sulfites, the wine may have naturally occurring sulfites, but the total sulfite level must be less than 20 parts per million. Labels use the phrase "contains sulfites" regardless of the approach.

Wine "Made with Organic Grapes" or "Made with Organically Grown Grapes"

Wines in these categories must be made from 100% organic grapes, but they can include added sulfites. In the case of yeast, this may or may not be organic. When the winery added sulfites, this wine is not considered organic even if the farming practices were organic.

Sustainable Viticultural Approaches

Some farmers take additional steps beyond standard organic winemaking to apply sustainable farming practices. Examples include the use of composting and the cultivation of specific plants to attract insects that are beneficial to the health of the vines. Sustainable practices in these vineyards also extend to actions that seem to have little or nothing to do with the production of grapes, such as providing areas for wildlife in order to prevent animals from eating the grapes. Sustainable practices also include allowing the growth of weeds and wildflowers between the vines. Sustainable farmers may use bio-diesel fuel for tractors in the vineyards to reduce emissions among the vines, plow with horses, and use solar energy.

Sustainable winemaking is a system with the perspective of integrating natural and human resources involving environmental health, economic profitability, as well as social and economic equity. Wineries participating in this oftentimes will add "SIP Certified" in their tasting rooms and on wine labels. This requires winemakers/wineries to take a small, realistic, and measurable step in their viticulture practices, as defined in the Code of Sustainable Winegrowing Practices Workbook published by the California Sustainable Winegrowing Alliance (CSWA).

Biodynamic Viticultural Approaches

Biodynamic viticulture stems from the ideas and suggestions of Rudolf Steiner (1861–1925). The principles and practices of biodynamics are based on his spiritual/practical philosophy, called anthroposophy, which includes understanding the ecological, the energetic and the spiritual in nature.

As a practical method of farming, biodynamics embody the ideal of ever-increasing ecological self-sufficiency, just as with modern agro-ecology, but includes ethical and spiritual considerations. This type of viticulture views the farm as a cohesive, interconnected living system. Biodynamic farming grows grapes with a strong connection to the healthy, living soil.
Biodynamic approaches conceive that the soil is a living organism, interconnected with every living organism on Earth, as well as connected with the moon and the planets. Farmers cannot only take away from the planet; farmers also have to nurture the soil by adding nutrients and energy. I realize for some people, this can be too much or too esoteric, but I have to say when I was in Chile, I lived on a small biodynamic farm, and the quality and taste of the fruit and vegetables I experienced as a result of these farming practices was just amazing.

Time to Make Some Wine!

As we can see, the only way to make a quality wine is to have quality fruit. So with this premise in mind, let's see how wine is made!

As grapes near maturity, the vineyard must be sampled to measure the sugar and acid levels. The grapes are usually tasted to evaluate the development of varietal flavor. Physiological ripeness (skin and pulp) and the phenolic ripeness (seeds) need to be at the most optimal level. Although sugar concentration can be measured in the vineyard, the fruit samples are usually brought into the winery's laboratory where sugar and acid can be measured more accurately. Sugar is measured either by its refraction of light with a retractometer used in the vineyard or the lab, or sugar can be measured by the density of the juice with a hydrometer. Acid is measured by titration and measurement of pH.

Generally in the U.S., the decision on when to harvest is based on the style of wine to be made and the desired alcohol concentration. This decision varies from winery to winery, and the AVA or TTB does not regulate when wineries should harvest. When grapes are at the most optimal stage of maturity is the time to harvest, at least in theory.

Monitoring the fruit regularly when close to harvest is very important. This way, the grape grower (viticulturist) or winemaker (enologist) checks the development of sugar Brix in the grapes, among the other elements. Grapes commonly used to be harvested between 23-25 on the Brix scale. What does this mean? If grapes are harvested at 24 sugar Brix, the alcohol level will be approximately 13.2%. If grapes are harvest at 26 sugar Brix, the alcohol level will be 14.3%, and so on. Here is the formula for obtaining alcohol level: Brix X 0.55 = alcohol level. So if the Brix is 24, let's plug our numbers in: 24 X 0.55 = 13.2% alcohol. Got it?!

Soon after harvest, the fruit is usually crushed. Some red wines are made with whole berry or whole cluster fermentations or a combination of both. Then, fermentation takes place before pressing, in the presence of skin and seeds. During red fermentations, the skin and some of the seeds form a cap that floats at the top of the tank. This layer is very thick and occupies about one-third of the total volume. Good extraction of color and tannins from the skin and seeds requires cap management and the regular mixing of the cap with the fermenting wine. In small fermenters like barrels, this can be accomplished simply by "punching down," pushing the cap down into the wine. In larger tanks, color extraction is accomplished by "pumping over," pumping wine from the bottom of the tank and spraying it over the surface of the cap until the cap is mixed back in. Punch downs or pump overs are typically performed twice a day during red wine fermentations; this frequency depends on each individual winery.

Fermentation temperatures in general are higher, 70° to 90° F, to ensure good color and tannin extraction, both of which are desirable in red wines, not so much or not at all in white wines. Red fermentation proceeds much faster, typically four to twelve days, compared to white wines, which take thirty or more days, because of the higher temperature and the better supply of nutrients for yeast provided by the skins and seeds, which is absent in white wines. Air contact is not such a great concern in red fermentation but is a big concern for white fermentation. Oxidation (browning) is not apparent in red wines; however, red juices contain natural antioxidants and the vigorous fermentation produces a dense surface layer of CO_2, preventing the air's entry, creating less browning. Many wineries use open-topped fermenters for red wines only.

Pigment (color) and tannin extraction are carefully managed in fermenting red wine by controlling the amount of skin contact. Both are increased by higher temperature, alcohol concentration, and by the amount of time (maceration) before pressing. Extraction is lowest in blush wines, which are pressed immediately after crushing. Rosé wines are pressed after twenty-four to thirty-six hours of skin contact. Red wines made in a light style are usually pressed after about four or five days. Premium red wines usually have longer skin contact, but the time can vary from ten to thirty days, long after fermentation has finished. Such extended maceration does not increase the color of the wine a whole lot because the color generally peaks after only four to eight days of skin contact. Extended time, however, does increase the tannin concentration of the wine, resulting in a wine that is more bitter and astringent. The degree of extraction of the phenolic color and astringent components is a key factor in red wine style, but this is not desirable in white wines. High tannin levels are associated with long aging but not necessarily all the time. If you have experienced drinking a young wine high in tannins, you know what I'm talking about. In order to make a wine that is ready to drink upon release, the tannin levels must be moderate and in balance with other key elements like sugar, acidity and fruit structure. It is very difficult to accomplish this without risking over-ripening the fruit and losing quality. Some wineries out there are more interested in fast winemaking due to financial considerations. Some wineries cannot afford to cellar and store wines for lengthy periods of time. It is important for you as a consumer to identify the wineries that focus on quality versus quantity in order to truly experience the pleasure of wine.

Lets take a look at the various techniques that some wineries use to reduce alcohol levels.

Enzyme Additions: Increase extraction and volatile aromatics

Yeast: Yeast is a key component in winemaking and in more traditional winemaking, wild/native yeast is used. Wild yeast is contained in the grape itself and lives in the cellar. Today, many wineries harvest their grapes with a high sugar content. As a result, it has become more common to use commercial yeast, which can have the strength to hold higher fermenting temperatures without risking death before fermentation is complete. The use of this new commercial yeast allows wineries to produce wines with high levels of alcohol—over 15% or 16% and in some cases even higher.

Reverse Osmosis: This is a technique commonly used to allow for effective and precise control of alcohol reduction. The industry has seen widespread acceptance of this method. In some circumstances in the use of reverse osmosis, other sensory compounds might also be removed, which could impact the wine's quality.

Water Dilution in Wine: These practices are regulated in most countries, with the total amount of added water not to exceed certain limits. Some wineries overripe the tannins which will result in heavy cellar manipulation in order to reduce alcohol levels, while other wineries leave the balancing act to Mother Nature. You may find yourself wondering, why not harvest earlier instead of diluting the wine? The answer to this question has a deeper root than we may think, but YOU as a consumer have a lot to do with it! I'll leave this question open for now and return to it in the winemaking part of the book.

Another way of making wine is fermenting grapes through the technique known as carbonic maceration. What is that?

Carbonic Maceration

This is a red wine variation in which whole berries are blanketed with CO_2 and left for approximately eight to ten days. During that time, chemical changes take place inside the berries, including the conversion of some sugar into alcohol. Eventually the skin breaks open and the juice, known as the "must," is pressed, inoculated, and allowed to ferment normally. This process produces a very fruity, low tannin, light red wine. It is used to produce nouveau ("new") wines that are released only a few weeks after harvest. The most famous of these is Beaujolais Nouveau from the Beaujolais region of France, which receives tremendous publicity each year when their wine is released simultaneously all over the world on the third Thursday in November. This winemaking technique is not only used for making Beaujolais Nouveau wines; today more and more maverick winemakers are applying carbonic maceration to multiple varieties of grapes, Pinot Noir or even Cabernet Sauvignons, for example. One interesting example of carbonic maceration winemaking is from Monsieur Louis-Antoine, a Frenchman living in Chile. Louis is making really interesting wines that capture the essence of Chilean *Terroir*.

Crushing

If you are not using the carbonic maceration technique, grapes need to be crushed in order to break them open ... thus making the juice accessible to the yeast. A crusher/de-stemmer usually performs this task. A crusher/de-stemmer is a horizontal device that breaks open the grapes and separates them from the cluster stem. The stems are usually separated, although this is a generalization, as some winemakers do partial de-stem, and other don't de-stem at all. Wines may also be made with whole clusters or the stems may be removed without crushing the whole grapes. Wines may also be created with a mixture of whole grapes and crushed grapes. The product of crushing, the must, consists of approximately 80% juice, 16% skins and 4% seeds. The pigment for red wines comes entirely from the skin. Approximately 70% of the tannins, which are important for flavor and aging, are found in the seeds and the rest of the tannins are derived from the stalks and skin. Thus, controlling the amount of contact between the juice, skins, and seeds is critical to controlling the flavor and color of the finished wine.

The Addition of Sulfur Dioxide, SO_2

After crushing, SO_2, (sulfur dioxide) is usually added to inhibit oxidation, which causes browning and other processes of deterioration, and also to inhibit growth of and to kill undesirable microorganisms. Although most wines contain added SO_2, sulfites are also produced naturally during fermentation and would be present to some degree even if SO_2 were not added. Wine sold in the U.S. must carry the phrase "contains sulfites" on the label if the concentration is above 10 parts per million (ppm) whether the concentration of SO_2 was enhanced or naturally occurring. Some wines are termed "organic wine," which is wine that is produced without added SO_2, but it will still contain naturally produced SO_2, usually at a concentration high enough to require the "contains sulfites" warning on the label. Some authorities say when sulfites are added to wine in large quantities, SO_2 can become a fault and has the potential to cause strong headaches.

Must Adjustment

Remember, "must" is the product of crushing of whole clusters which contain the seeds, pulp, and skin all mixed together. If the potential alcohol concentration of the must is too low, which is not very common in California, it may be enriched by the addition of concentrated grape juice or, in some cases, the addition of sugar, known as "chaptalization". Chaptalization is prohibited in California, as well as in southern Europe and in other locales around the world. In California, we are allowed to use grape juice for must adjustment. Wineries may also need to adjust acidity, among other things, for grapes that are lacking in tannins, for example. In California, acidity is more often too low than too high and is adjusted by the addition of tartaric acid in the form of powder to the juice (the must).

Pressing

Pressing is done in order to separate the juice or wine from the skins and seeds. It may take place before fermentation, as with white and blush wines, or after fermentation, in the case of red wines. Juice or wine that drains away from the skins and seeds by gravity alone, without added pressure, is called "free run" and is typically about 80 to 90% of the juice or wine volume. It is relatively low in tannins and is considered to have the highest quality. Additional press fractions are obtained by applying a hard press. Press fractions may be kept separate and used for different purposes; the hard press sometimes is sold for bulk wine or distillation. The residue of skins and seeds that remains after pressing is called pomace. Many wineries will spread the pomace in the vineyards as a natural, organic compound. This practice can also encourage a stronger presence of wild yeast in the vineyard. One ton of grapes typically yields 140 to 190 gallons of juice or wine. Red grapes yield more than white grapes, with an average of 175 gallons per ton versus 150 gallons per ton for white grapes, approximately. This is because red grapes are pressed after fermentation, when liquid can be more fully extracted. Also, red wine can be pressed harder because the tannin concentration increases as more pressure is applied to the seeds and skins. In contrast, this is not desirable in white wines because crispiness and fruitiness are more desirable than bitter and tannic characteristics.

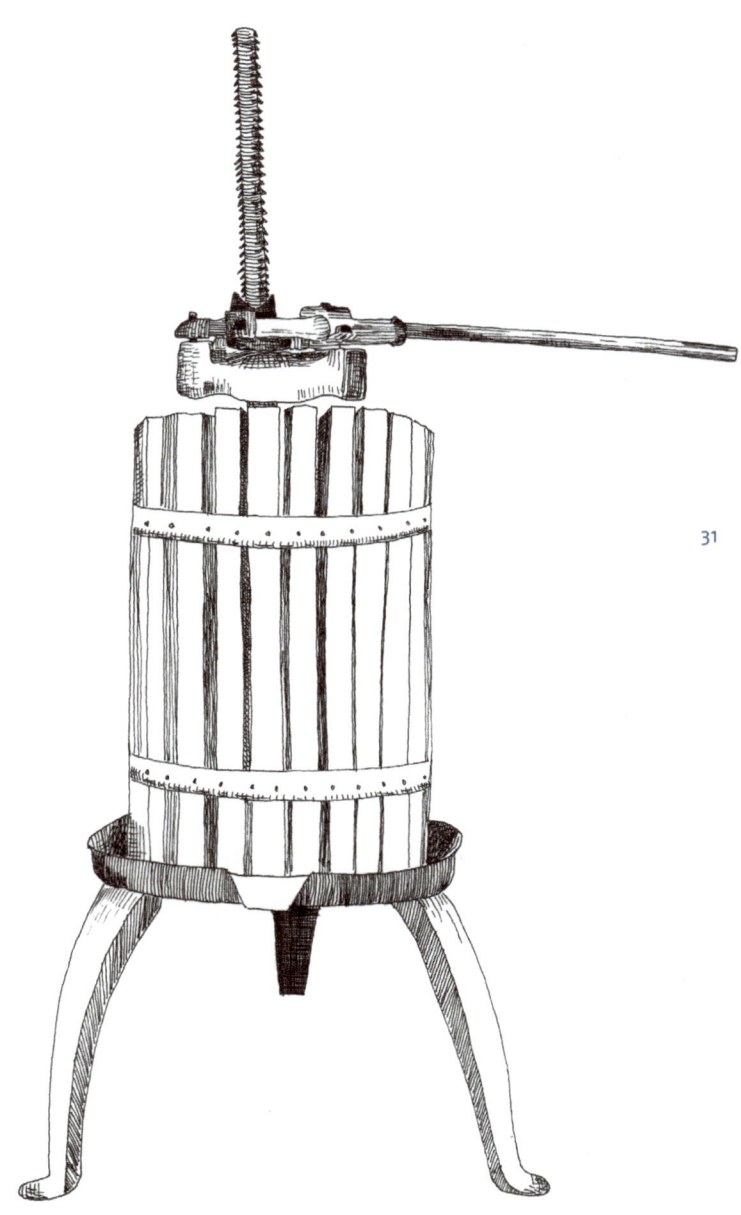

Basket press

Types of Presses

Probably one of the simplest and oldest types of press is the basket press. This press consists of a piston within a cylinder made of wooden slats which pushes the fruit down. The juice runs out through the spaces between the slats. Even today, many small wineries use this type of press. Modern presses include the moving head press (a horizontal piston device), and the screw press, where skins and seeds are added in one end and subjected to increasing pressure as they are moved along inside by a metal screw. Typically, these two types of presses are found in medium and large wineries.

The most widely used press in medium to large premium wineries around the world is the membrane or bladder press. For this press, a rubber bladder, similar to a balloon, lines the inside of the press. Pressure exerted by the bladder forces air to press against the fruit. The pressure is extremely gentle, making this a very efficient method of extracting wine because it can take place without excessive skin and seed breakage, which would increase the tannin concentration in the wine.

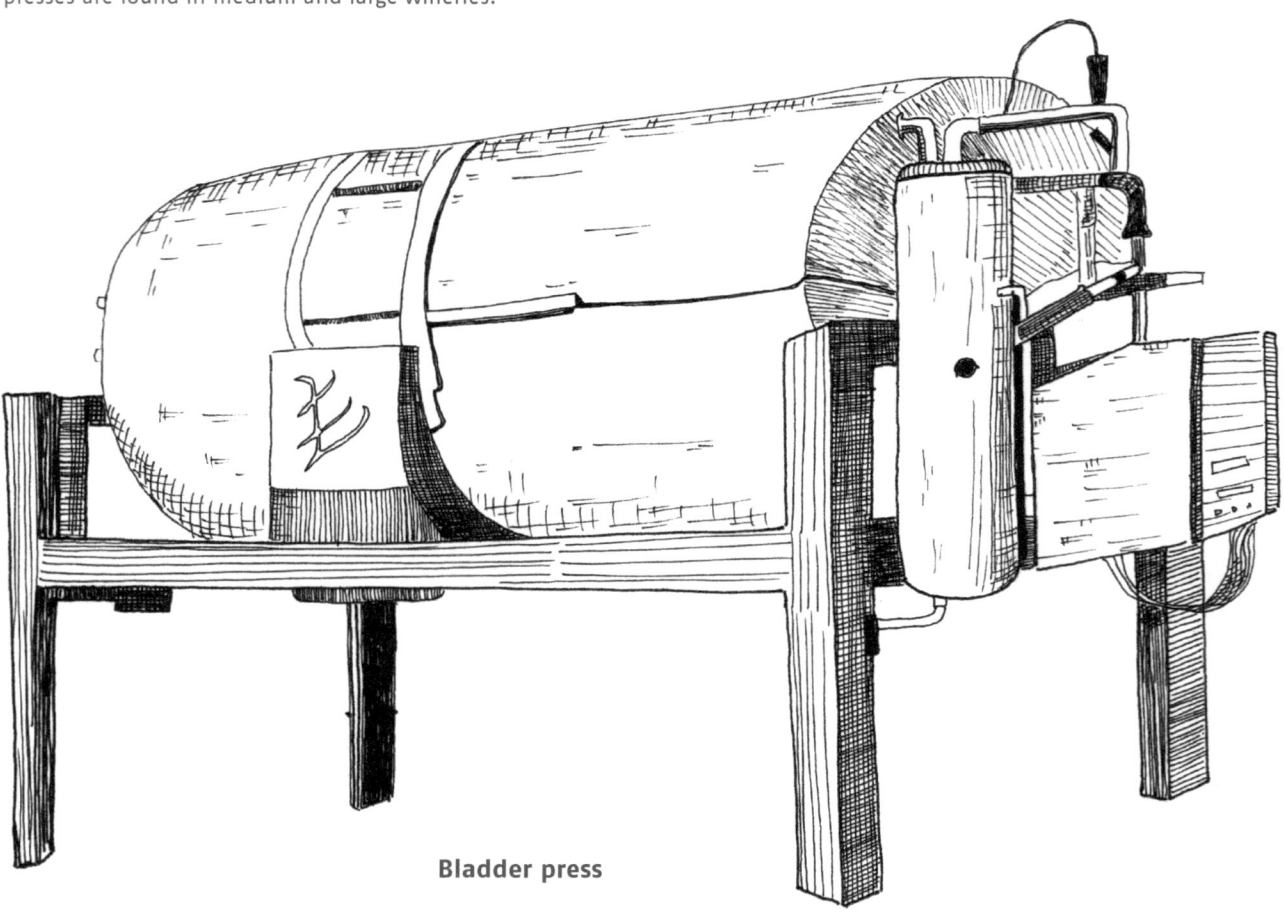

Bladder press

Racking and Lees

Racking: Wine from the press contains some suspended solid material that is allowed to settle to the bottom of the tank. This material is known as "lees." The process of transferring the wine away from settled solid material (lees) is called racking. Racking can be done three or four times before the wine is clear.

Lees: This material consists of fruit solids, dead yeast or chemical precipitates. Alternatively, the solids may be removed by filtration or centrifugation. Filtration and/or centrifugation are more commonly used in large wineries, as opposed to boutique and garage wineries where unfined and unfiltered wines are a common practice. This is all generally speaking, as sometimes large wineries don't filter or unfine the wine, and sometimes small wineries filter or centrifuge their wines. Just because a winery is small doesn't automatically imply their practices are artisan and similarly, some large wineries have artisan practices in place. I appreciate the artisan approach because this practice preserves the wine's integrity and doesn't take away complexity. Some wineries do little to almost nothing to educate their patrons/consumers about the meaning of these practices. I believe this is a missed marketing opportunity! Perhaps wine already seems confusing enough for the consumer ... but I think the more you educate your consumers, the better.

Fermentation

In commercial types of winemaking, fermentation is usually initiated by inoculating or adding the juice or must with cultured yeast at a concentration of 1–2% by volume. Some winemakers choose not to inoculate and rely on the yeast that is naturally present in the grapes, also known as wild and/or natural yeast. This tendency is increasingly popular among many winemakers, particularly the boutique and garage-style wineries. Many different kinds of vessels can be used as fermenters: wooden tanks, plastic boxes, concrete tanks lined with or without epoxy, clay amphora, and the most common style among modern wineries today, stainless steel tanks. Although open-topped fermenters are often used for red wine, fermentation vessels for white wine should always have a top to exclude air and contaminants. In the case of white wine, steel tanks are more commonly used, but today I observe and taste white wines fermented in concrete and amphorae and the results are great wines!

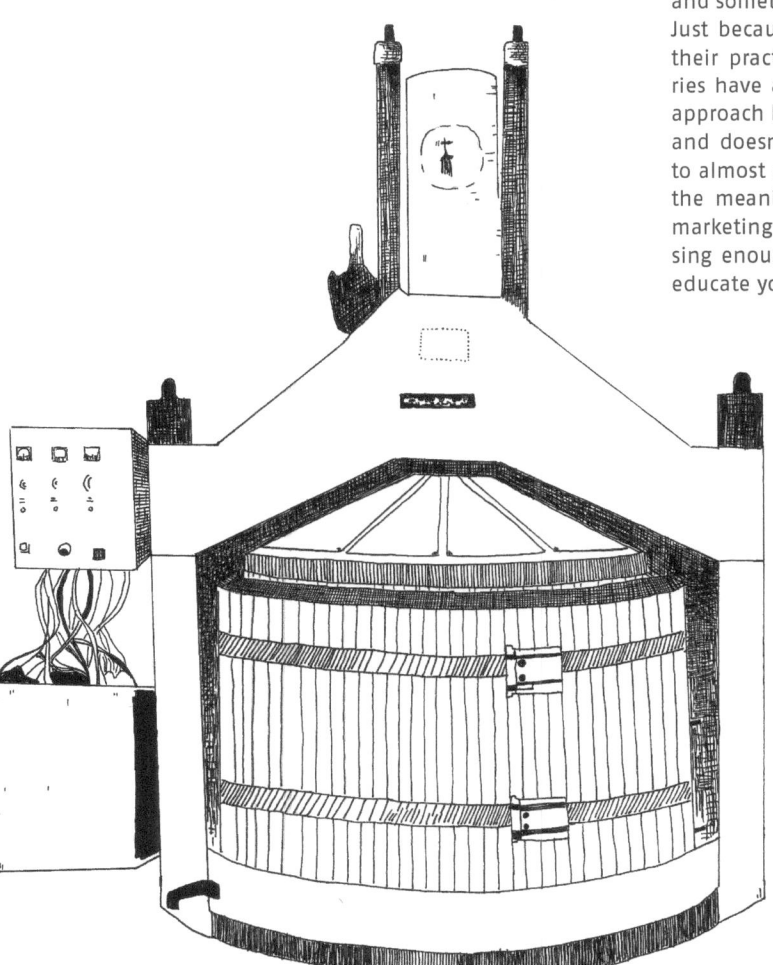

Modern electric press

Managing the Fermentation

When wineries are small and rustic, they need to manage the fermentation very closely. Temperature must be managed because the fermentation of ripe grapes can raise the temperature of a fermentation vessel above the upper limit for yeast, and also because fermentation temperatures influence wine flavors. Heat is more readily dissipated from small fermenters because of their relatively large surface-to-volume ratio. In medium and large wineries, heat is most commonly controlled by the use of stainless steel tanks that have refrigeration jackets or by heat exchangers to cool the fermentation. This type of vessel is expensive and requires a big investment.

The CO_2 produced during fermentation must also be accommodated by allowing excess CO_2 pressure to be released through a fermentation lock on the fermenter, allowing CO_2 to escape while preventing the entry of air. Recently emptied fermenters are full of CO_2 and winery workers must enter these tanks to shovel out the last of the skins and seeds (for red fermentation). Workers going to the press must take precautions to avoid suffocating. Today some wineries are paying closer attention to controlling CO_2 emissions by integrating new technologies aimed at protecting employees and the environment.

White Wine Fermentation

White wines are typically fermented at lower temperatures, 55°F to 70°F, than red wines (70°F to 90°F). White fermentations take much longer than red fermentations, ten to thirty days versus four to twelve days, respectively. This is in part because they are conducted at lower temperatures and also because they do not contain the skins, seeds, and other solid material that can provide food, nutrients, and attachment surfaces for yeast. Some white varieties ferment faster than others, presumably because they are a better source of certain yeast nutrients.

What happens if fermentation stops?

"Stuck fermentation" is the name given to the fermentation process when it stops before all the fermentable sugar is gone or "eaten" by the yeast. This results in a wine that is sweet and microbiologically unstable. So, in order to assist the wine to finalize fermentation, the process may be restarted by adding yeast nutrients or heating/cooling the must. The result will be a dry wine that, afterwards, you and I will finally enjoy!

The Famous Malolactic Fermentation (MLF)

Malolactic fermentation is a secondary fermentation process that usually occurs when wine is in barrels. In this process, the malic and tartaric acids are transformed into lactic acid. Think tart green apples versus yogurt, butter, or milk/cream, making the wine more subtle and creamy in texture. Probably the clearest example of that creamy and buttery texture on the palate is certain Chardonnays. If you have yet to experience what I'm talking about, you should to run and visit a tasting room as soon as possible and ask to taste a Chardonnay! Typically, wineries make them in different styles, so good luck in your exploration!

Barrel Aging

Aging wine in oak barrels adds tertiary aromas and flavors to wine, such as vanilla, spicy, and occasionally a smoky flavor, if the barrel has been medium to heavily toasted. *See tertiary aromas chart, pg. 40.* Most premium red wines are barrel aged for a minimum of six months to two years on average, but there are some cases where red wines can easily be aged three or more years in barrels. This is common in Spain. White wine is aged in barrels little, if at all. Wines intended to have a fruity flavor, whether they are red, white, or blush, are not barrel aged. Barrel aging is very costly because oak barrels are very expensive, $900 to $1,200 each depending on if the barrel is American or French oak. French barrels usually are the most expensive. A traditional oak barrel holds 220 liters, about 58 gallons.

Although French oak barrels have been the most popular with California premium winemakers, American oak is being used increasingly, not only because it is much less expensive, but also because refinements in barrel production (coopering) have shown that American oak can produce fine wine flavors. An example of that is Ridge Winery. The flavor contribution of a barrel declines with repeated use and a barrel typically lasts for five years if it is French oak and up to ten years for American oak. A winery typically uses a mixture of new and older barrels and replaces the older barrels after a few years. A batch of wine is often divided up, some going into new barrels and some into older barrels. "Neutral barrels" are those that have previously been used at least three or more times. These divisions will be blended back together at the end of the winemaking process.

Wine evaporates from barrels so they must be regularly topped off to replace the lost wine and eliminate air space that can permit the development of volatile acidity (acetic acid and ethyl acetate) caused by a bacterium called acetobacter. Wine is periodically racked from barrel to barrel, which eventually clarifies it, and it may also be treated with SO_2 during and after barrel aging. This process happens within conventional wineries; organic wines do not add extra sulfites. Some wineries with a so-called "natural approach" don't add many, if any, sulfites.

What happens when barrels are not an option?

As an inexpensive alternative to oak barrels, winemakers sometimes use pieces of oak that can be placed inside a stainless steel tank, or they may use oak chips. Both allow the development of some oak flavors in the wine but at a much lower cost.

Fining

Fining is a method of clarifying wine. Despite being racked (manually clarified), wine may still be hazy because of protein, residual dead yeast, or microbial residues. So many wineries use different types of treatments to clarify the wine, with some treatments being more invasive then others. Also, if the wine has excessive tannins, some winemakers will remove them by treating the wine with a fining agent that, when mixed with the wine, reacts with and absorbs the substance which then precipitates out and falls to the bottom of the vessel or barrel. The wine can then be racked to remove the substance. Sometimes animal products are used, like egg whites, gelatin, and casein (milk protein). All remove tannins and other phenolic substances. Bentonite, a type of clay, removes protein hazes, and certain enzymes will break down/remove polysaccharides (sugars). Fining improves the clarity of wine, but excessive fining my also eliminate components that contribute to the complexity and wine flavor. As I mentioned before, some wineries use egg whites or other substances derived from animals to clarify their wines. It is important that vegan consumers take caution in that respect. Ask the winery if they're using animal products or not. Also ask if they follow the more common process of clarification (described below) or if their approach is more natural.

Tartrate Stabilization

Probably some of you have had the experience of buying a bottle of wine that you left in the refrigerator and then perhaps forgot about it for at least a few days or maybe even weeks! The wine remains in there for awhile, or maybe you left it in the garage during winter and forgot about it. Unexpectedly, you receive a text or phone call from this family member that you adore, or maybe your best friend, announcing with very short notice their visit from out-of-town. So here we go ... finally the family member or friend arrives and you decide to make a nice dinner. The night is fabulous, fun, and at some point, you drink all the wine and it is too late to go to the store. Suddenly you remember this neglected bottle and decide to open it. This forgotten bottle appears as a savior from heaven. So, as happy as a college student who suddenly finds a $20 bill in his pants pocket while doing laundry, you proceed to open the miracle bottle. To your surprise, you find little crystals in the wine. At this point you probably exclaim, "WHAT THE HECK," among other thing I can't express in this book out of respect to my audience. So with a lot of anger and sadness, you decide to dump the neglected bottle of vino down the drain. Unfortunately, no sommelier was there to counsel you and say, "STOP! Don't you worry; you can drink this wine with no problem. Those are only tartrates which form when there is an abrupt change in temperature and the potassium and tartaric acid in wine forms a crystalline precipitate called potassium acid tartrate, (KHT).

These crystals can alarm consumers, as you were alarmed, because they may think it is an impurity or they may even mistake the crystals for broken glass. Some wineries prevent the formation of crystals by cold stabilization. What exactly is cold stabilization? Basically it is chilling the wine below 32°F for several weeks to cause the KHT to precipitate. Then, racking or filtration can remove it before the wine is bottled. So what is the lesson? Next time you see particles that look like glass or crystals, drink the wine. Voila!

To Filter or Not to Filter

The practice of filtering is more common in large wineries due to the fact that filtering allows stability, consistency, and more predictability in terms of flavor. In order to accomplish this, the wine may be further clarified and stabilized by passing it through various filters. This type of filtration tool is used to remove particulate matter. Any microbes that may lead to problems with microbial instability in the bottle can be removed by sterile filtration. Sterile filtration is especially important in wine containing residual sugar that could serve as a food for remaining yeast cells. Filtration is also important in wine that has not undergone malolactic fermentation. Why? The wine bottle could, later, undergo malolactic fermentation where malolactic bacteria are present. With excessive fining and excessive filtration, this can reduce the flavor and complexity of a fine wine. Many premium wineries minimize filtration, or even avoid it altogether.

The Art of Blending

Just as a painter or musician can compose and create a terrific painting or a killer song, this is the point where the winemaker's skills can blossom. Creativity, palate, and experience take flight to create a magnificent, seductive piece of art in the form of wine. To facilitate this creative process, a winery may produce separate wines from a variety of vineyards, different fruit maturities, and even from different winemaking treatments. These may be blended to produce a balanced wine. Typically, different proportions of components are mixed together and tasted on a very small scale in order to determine the final full-scale blend proportions. I will say this is why some people think winemakers practice a form of art when making amazing wines. Blending requires an excellent palate as well as enough experience to be able to project the wine in the future. Wines have the potential to offer excitement, complexity, and can blow your socks off!!! To accomplish this, my friends, is not easy!

Ready for Bottling

Ready to bottle? Let's do it! Bottles are usually turned upside down and rinsed with hot water just before they are filled. Some winemakers may also "sparge" (sprinkle) with nitrogen. A cork is inserted into the bottle immediately after it is filled. If the fill volume has been correctly adjusted, there will be minimal head-space, the air space between the top of the wine and the bottom of the cork. The label is then applied to the bottle, which can be a tedious process as I learned from hand-labeling bottles! After labeling, the bottles are then placed into case boxes. These are then stacked and stored to allow bottle aging, a few months for whites and up to two years for some reds. Alternatively, the labels may be applied after bottle aging if the bottles are to be stored in a humid cellar that might damage the labels. This is a common practice with cave aged wines and champagne. During the stage of bottle aging, the wine can be further monitored to detect any instability problems.

It is very common for some small wineries not to have their own bottling system, so an external company provides this service.

Red Wine Process

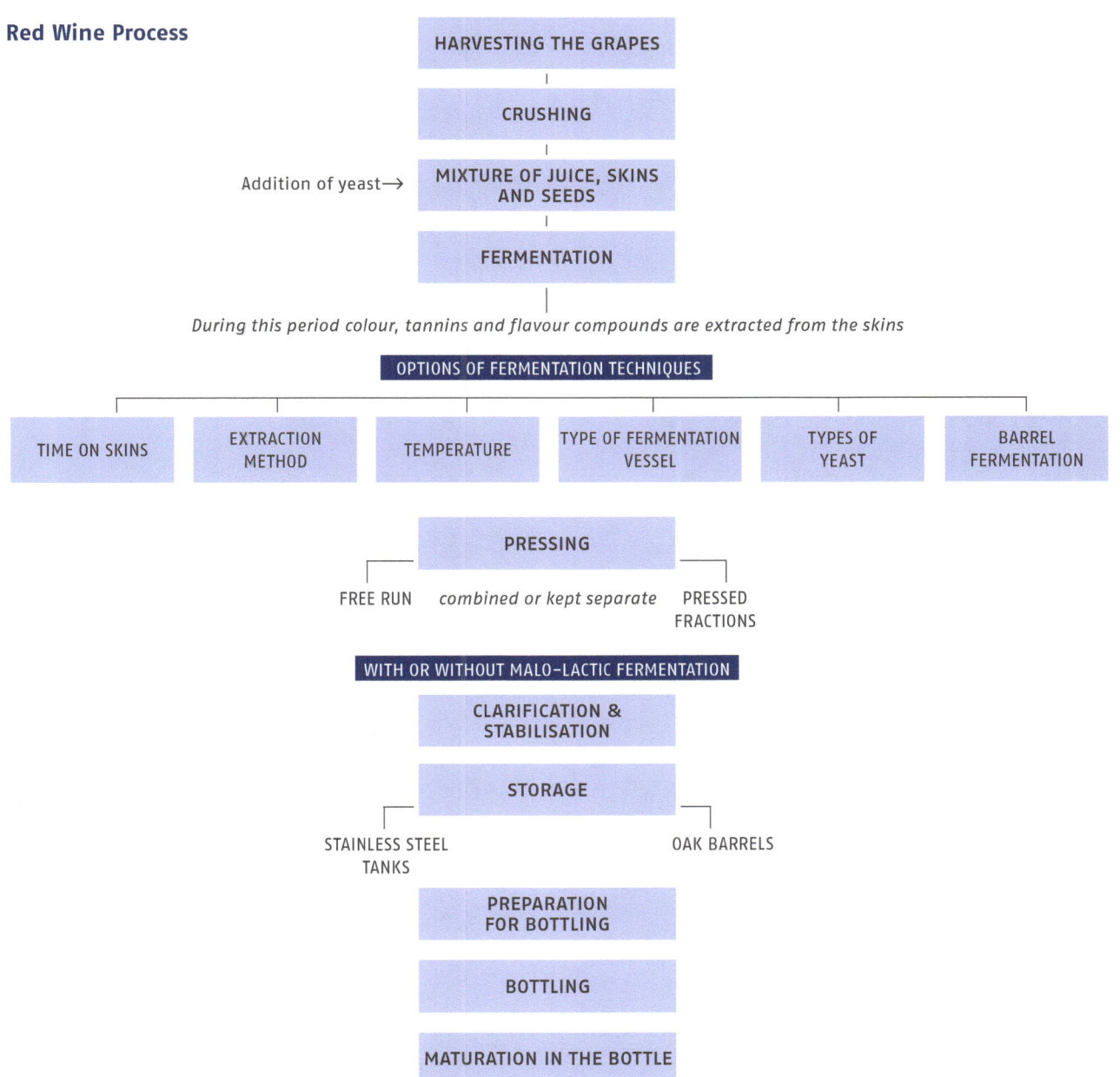

Making White Wines

After crushing, the must is sometimes allowed to settle in a drain tank to permit juice to drain away by gravity. Peptic enzymes may be added to help break down the fruit tissue and release more juice. The juice is kept cold and protected from air to prevent the browning caused by the oxidation of phenolic compounds. The must is pressed right away to minimize the extraction of phenolic compounds (which include tannins) from the skins and seeds. Phenolic compounds are undesirable in white wines, not only because they are the substrate for browning, but also because they contribute bitterness and astringency, harsh flavors that are usually undesirable in white wines. White grapes are sometimes sent directly to press without crushing, which reduces the phenolics even further. After pressing, the juice is allowed to settle in a refrigerated tank, raked off the juice lees, and inoculated. (Note: Chardonnay that is to be barrel fermented would be pumped into barrels at this point.)

Most white wines are fermented in temperature-controlled tanks in which the temperature is kept relatively low, 55°F to 70°F to maximize the fruity flavors that are produced by yeast at low temperatures, and to minimize the loss of volatile flavor compounds that can occur with rapid CO_2 generation at higher temperatures. Low temperature and scarcity of yeast nutrients (because the skins and seeds are absent) results in a relatively long fermentation time, ten to thirty days, compared to red wines.

Barrel Fermentation

Some white wines, particularly premium Chardonnays and occasionally other varieties like Sauvignon Blanc, are barrel fermented and usually undergo malolactic fermentation at the same time. Barrel-fermented Chardonnays have characteristic flavors of vanilla from the oak, and butter, from diacetyl produced by the MLF bacteria. Although the barrels are not temperature-controlled, their small volume allows heat dissipation and keeps the fermentation temperature low. After fermentation, the wine may be left in barrels for up to six months to undergo sur lie aging, (aging on the lees). During this time, flavors are contributed by dead and dying yeast and this may be enhanced by stirring the barrels regularly, which contributes to a creamy texture to the wine. Barrel fermentation is used only for expensive wines because both the barrels and the labor required are costly, as mentioned above.

White wines can be made both dry or sweet. Premium Chardonnays and most Sauvignon Blancs are made dry. Less expensive Chardonnays are often made with small amounts of residual sugar. Fruity varieties like Riesling, Gewürztraminer and Chenin Blanc are often made in a slightly sweet style. The sweet characteristic may be produced from arresting the fermentation (by chilling or sterile filtration) before all the sugar is consumed, or by fermenting to dryness and adding sterile juice concentrate.

White Wine Process

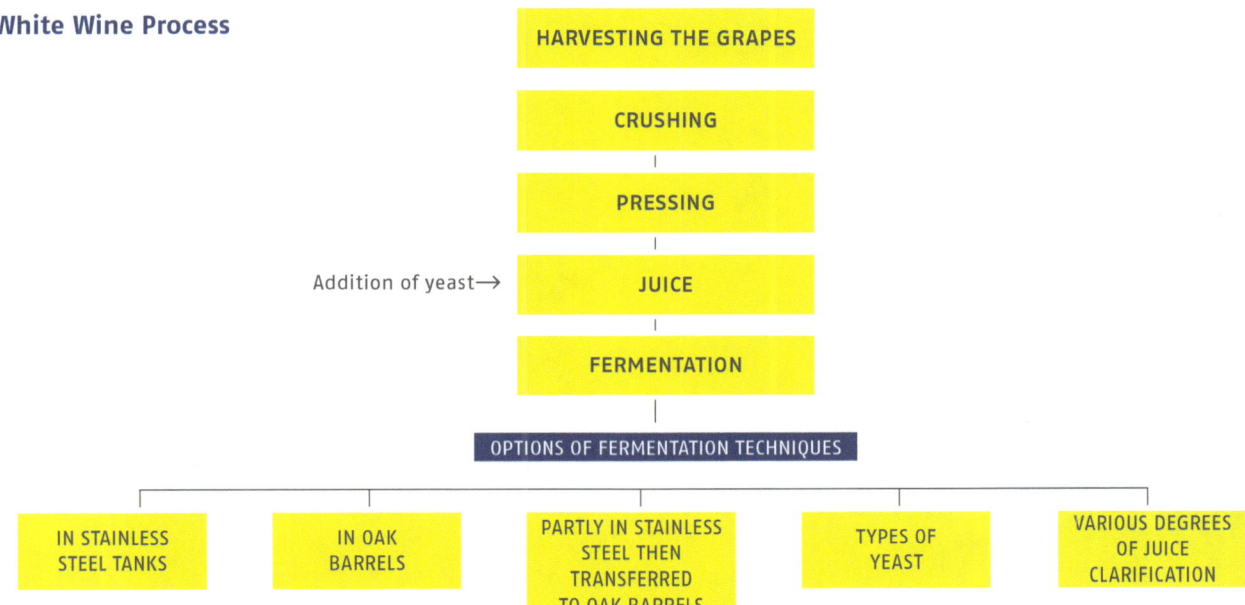

with or without malo-lactic fermentation and/or with or without yeast lees contact with the wine after fermentation is complete

As we see, for the most part the quality of the wine will be determined by the quality of the fruit. The winemaker must work very hard to not interrupt the expression of nature, so eventually their work can become invisible. As parents guide their child to blossom beautifully, the winemaker has an important role in guiding the process for wines to blossom ... or not. Let's take a look at some of the fundamental decisions a winemaker must consider:

. When to harvest?

. Level of sugar Brix?

. Level of grape maturity (physiological and phenolic)

. How to harvest, by hand or machine?

. Crush? De-stem? Whole berries? Whole clusters?

. Add SO2 or not? If so, how much?

. Add juice concentrate?

. Adjust acid?

. Natural wild yeast or commercial yeast fermentation?

. Size and type of fermentation vessel? Wood, cement, steel, clay?

. Fermentation temperature?

. Alcohol reduction

. Type of press? Free run, basket press, membrane press?

. Barrel aging? Type of oak? French, American, Hungarian, or something else? How much to toast the barrel? Light, medium, or fully toasted?

. What percentage of wine to age in new barrels?

. How often to rack barrels?

. Fining? With what? How much? Using or not using animal products?

. Filter or not to filter? "Wineshakespeare?"

. Cold stabilization? Ion exchange (getting fancy and nerdy)?

. Adjust alcohol?

. How long to bottle age? (Most of the time this is a commercial decision rather than a decision made for the goodness of the wine.)

. When to release?

. How much to charge?

. Design of the labels, modern or Old World? How much information on the label (besides the legal requirements)?

The Role of the Consumer and Media in High Octane Wine

There has been a trend over recent decades here in the U.S. toward wines with a higher concentration of alcohol. This trend can be linked to greater consumer acceptance for certain wine styles. On the other hand, the media is a big influence, having the tendency to prefer wine higher in alcohol. The scoring system in many cases reflects their choice. Another factor to consider is that growing quality grapes in warmer and drier climates has led to wines that are rich and full-bodied with ripe fruit flavor profiles. In general, warm, dry, climates minimize fruit deterioration, according to viticulturists, and allow winemakers flexibility in choosing when to harvest. As we all know, here in California we are privileged with excellent weather conditions, and I personally experience that all the time living in Monterey. This flexibility facilitates production of wines with a greater range of flavor styles, many of them with high levels of alcohol and very fruity characteristics. Having fruity characteristics is not necessarily bad, but many times wines are intentionally designed this way because wineries are looking for a good score. Inevitably this practice puts typicity, the degree a wine reflects its varietal origins, at risk. The decision to extend the time before harvest, according to the winemaker, is to reduce green characters in the grape and to enhance the preferred flavor profile of wines. Also this decision to harvest late might lead to higher sugar concentrations. This in turn leads to wines with high levels of alcohol, which is not necessarily bad when alcohol is well integrated and in balance. Remember, we saw and learned in the winemaking process that in some cases, high alcohol levels can negatively affect wine flavor and complexity of the wine. An example of this is when you TASTE wines that give you a "hot" or burning sensation after tasting ... this, in my opinion, is not really appealing. I have to say I believe there are wines for any occasion; some you may want to drink as an apéritif or without food, but the level of alcohol of some wines is just incredible! I'm referring to wines over 16% alcohol. Also, elevated percentages of alcohol increase costs in countries where taxes are levied according to alcohol concentration, which is the case of the U.S. When wines pass 14% alcohol, another more costly taxation takes place.

Blockbuster Wines

The tendency of wineries trying to satisfy the media and certain wine writers creates a whole category of wines known worldwide as "blockbuster wines." With this type of winemaking philosophy, wines become very generic and lose their sense of place, identity, and sex appeal. This loss of identity makes it difficult to distinguish the difference between regions where typicity should add uniqueness to a wine and region. Fortunately, the tendency to produce generic wines has been changing due to many factors. Certainly one I observe is the new generation of winemakers around the world who are committed to making regionally unique wines. In California many new generation winemakers are following in the footsteps of rebel winemakers from the 1980s and 90s like Paul Drake (Ridge), Jim Clendensen (The Aubon Climat), and Randall Grahm. From a media standpoint, these winemakers were not very popular at the time, but today they are becoming more and more influential among the new generation of winemakers, and finally gaining their well-deserved recognition. Another reason I believe change is taking place is the new confidence consumers are beginning to have, in addition to the availability of information in blogs and social media. These outlets help consumers have easy access to information and influence consumers to take part in the wine conversation. I caution you to be careful with the integrity and legitimacy of the source where you get your information. If you want to find out more about the new generation of winemakers and wineries in California, I strongly recommend the book The New California Wine by Jon Bonné.

Finally, I also observe an exciting trend of more wine professionals involved in all spectrums of the hospitality industry and beyond. This is really an awesome time in the world of wine, salud to that!

02

Awareness of the Senses

The senses are one of the most important characteristics for us as human beings. With them we can differentiate thousands of different aromas, textures, and sensations. With them you can TASTE the world around us.

This chapter focuses primarily on unveiling the complexities of the aromatic nuances in wine, how those aromas develop and what is involved when you smell a wine. This chapter will not only guide you on how to taste wine, but also can be used as a tasting guide to basically any other beverage.

Where Are the Aromas and Flavors Coming From?

Our capabilities as humans to identify aromas are not so amazing compared to those of animals. Maybe that's the reason my ex-wife liked her cats better than me, but perhaps this little detail of my life that I'm sharing with you in this book is more information than you care to know. Still very amazingly, our senses can identify thousands of different aromas, but, my friends, better start paying attention and using your senses fully, so besides becoming a good wine taster, you can be more attractive to your girlfriend, wife or lover.

More seriously, my general experiences working in the wine industry have led me to discover a commonly misunderstood concept: aroma development. For instance, there are a lot of assumptions that fruit is blended in wine; either that, or the person who wrote the tasting notes has some source of special powers like Darth Vader.

Like every discipline in life, appropriate training and practice certainly can make you a master of tasting. In the wine world, there is no such thing as special powers, only a lot of discipline and practice. If you add reading and traveling, your skill will be even better. The more you taste and explore different regions and varieties of wine, the more of an expert you will be. To help you with that, you need to know the three main sources of flavors.

Main Sources of Flavors in Wine:

1. The grapes (Primary Aromas)
2. Fermentation (Secondary Aromas)
3. Processing and aging of the wine (Tertiary aromas)

Let us further explore these sources of aromas!

Primary Aromas *(varietal aromas)*

These aromas originate in the grapes and vary according to the vine, terroir, and climate. Primary aromas, for the most part, cover the fruity and floral nuances. They are an expression of viticulture ... that is why a Pinot Noir from Burgundy, France, will taste and have different aromatic nuances than a Pinot Noir from the Santa Lucia Highlands along California's Central Coast. This is called a "sense of a place," or typicity, and personally I love that! I don't expect a Burgundy Pinot Noir to taste like a Santa Lucia Highlands Pinot Noir or vice-versa. I think this is the beauty of each terroir and the real identity of every place expressed in a bottle of wine.

Secondary Aromas *(pre-fermentation and fermentation)*

These come about in both alcoholic and malolactic fermentations. They vary according to maceration time, fermentation temperatures, and the type of yeast used and their strains, wild yeast or commercial. They are a result of winemaking, the degree of influence and manipulation the winemaker is going to add during the process. There is a saying in the wine industry, "If you don't have good grapes, your chances of making a good wine are very limited or realistically impossible." However, even with great grapes, winemakers can produce a poor wine depending on their skills and style of winemaking.

Tertiary Aromas *(Post-fermentation and maturing)*

Have you ever wondered where aromas such as vanilla, coffee, toast or chocolate come from? Well, those are the aromas coming from the barrel! Remember, barrels are caramelized inside (toasted), and will add a woody, toasty, and caramel aroma to the wine. Yes, those are the tertiary aromas coming from barrel maturing and aging. Also remember, once the wine is in the bottle it will continue evolving. Wine is a living thing, evolving every day, week, month and year, like a child ... how awesome is that!

The Senses

Are we really using our senses?

I learned from teaching classes and working in tasting rooms that one of the biggest concerns people have is the notion that tasting wine is very difficult. I believe this is based on assumptions that people who write about wine and wine professionals (sommeliers) have an extraordinary and almost inhuman ability to taste wines, compared to a regular consumer. This is certainly superstition rather than reality. Actually, all of us have the same capabilities (with some exceptions), but the problem lies in the misuse of the senses.

How is that?

The style of life that revolves around so-called "modern society" means many people are connected to devices and living in a rush. This lifestyle blocks the senses due to constant internal/external noise. For instance, eating and drinking in front of the TV, in a car, or conversing in a loud environment, drinking coffee with the lid on the cup, eating in restaurants that rush you (not necessarily fast-food restaurants), sharing a table yet not interacting with the people you are face-to-face with due to interacting with devices, etc. All the constant distractions and disconnections with the senses prohibit people from experiencing the real joy of a glass of wine, the real joy of a meal, the real joy of a cup of coffee, or perhaps the real joy of a face-to-face conversation.

The good news is that you can transform habits! Yes, it takes some work but you can change habits that are blocking you from truly experiencing real joy and connection with your food, drink and people. Sensory awareness with something as intimate as putting food in your mouth requires full attention and total connection to your senses, both of which bring real joy as opposed to just the mechanical action of eating for the sake of filling the tummy. I challenge you to start enjoying and exciting all of your senses!

Lets see how the sensory system works!

As human beings, we have a sophisticated system in our brain that helps us recognize and identify hundreds of aromas. There is a gland in our brain called the thalamus. This gland stores memories of aromas that we collect from the time we were babies onward. So when we smell anything like dirt, flowers, fruit, cat pee, wet dog, etc., we store the aromatic memory unconsciously and/or consciously in the thalamus gland. In the particular situation or experience of tasting wine, when our nose smells the wine, minuscule and invisible molecules are directly passing from our nasal passage (guided by mucus) to our brain. This triggers memories of aromatic scents that we have been collecting in our personal history of life since we were born. That said, our ability to identify primary aromas will depend on how frequently we taste a particular variety of wine. In time, even in a blind taste test context, we will be able to identify the wine because we have been tasting that particular variety so many times that we recognize the character profiles (flavors) of the variety relatively easily.

In the case of the tertiary aromas, those come from the barrel and as I mentioned before, barrels are toasted inside. While the wine ages in the barrel, it is going to extract different flavor notes from the barrel. Usually you will hear people describing flavors like vanilla, cedar, coconut, clove, butter, toasted almonds, toasted hazelnut, caramel, coffee, and smoke, to mention just a few. Now the question is, how do these aromas originate? The scientific answer is:

Creamy Characters in Wine

Aroma	Compound	Resulting From
Butter	Diacetyl	Lactic bacteria and malolactic fermentation
Cream	Diacetyl	Lactic bacteria and malolactic fermentation

Vanilla and Nut Aromas in Wine

Aroma	Compound	Resulting From
Vanilla	Benzadehyde	Degree of toasting of the barrel or chips
Toasted almonds	Benzadehyde	Degree of toasting of the barrel or chips
Toasted hazelnuts	Benzadehyde	Degree of toasting of the barrel or chips

Coconut and Woody Aromas in Wine

Aroma	Compound	Resulting From
Coconut	Cis-methyl-octalactone	Hydrolyzed from barrel
Wood	Cis-methyl-octalactone	Affected by degree of toasting

Spicy Aromatic Nuances in Wine

Aroma	Compound	Resulting From
Cloves	Eugenol	Metabolism of phenolic acids coming from grape and wood by yeast and lactic bacteria
Smoke	4-ethyl-guaiacol	Metabolism of phenolic acids coming from grape and wood by yeast and lactic bacteria
Toasted Bread	Eugenol	Metabolism of phenolic acids coming from grape and wood by yeast and lactic bacteria
White and black pepper	Eugenol	Metabolism of phenolic acids coming from grape and wood by yeast and lactic bacteria

According to science, secondary aromas develop during fermentation. Chemical compounds that mimic nuances of fruits will develop as a result of fermentation. Let's take a look at some examples:

Fruity and Floral Aromas in White Wine

Aroma	Compound	Resulting From
Fruity	3-methyl-l-butyl acetate	Carbonic maceration and thermo-vinification
Banana	3-methyl-l-butyl acetate	Carbonic maceration and thermo-vinification
Pineapple	3-methyl-l-butyl acetate	Carbonic maceration and thermo-vinification
Flowers	Esters	Fermentation

Fruity and Floral Aromas in Red Wine

Aroma	Compound	Resulting From
Bell Pepper	Pyrazines	Physiological characteristic of varieties like Cabernet Franc, Cabernet Sauvignon (the presence is determined by viticultural management and winemaking)
Asparagus	Pyrazines	Physiological characteristic of varieties like Cabernet Franc, Cabernet Sauvignon (the presence is determined by viticultural management and winemaking)
Raspberry	Esters	Fermentation
Strawberry	Esters	Fermentation
Flowers	Esters	Fermentation

It is important to know for you as a consumer that all wines are not created equal. Some wines are crafted with a lot of dedication, attention, and, even though it can sound cliché, some producers put a lot of love and passion into the production of their wines. Similar to life, however, things are not always perfect and wine occasionally presents some faults. Reasons? Most faults occur because wines are not stored properly, bad hygiene in the winery, or the wine has been poorly made in the winery. Let's take a look to some of the most common flaws in wine:

Most Common Faulty Aromas

Aroma	*Compound*	*Resulting From*
Cork	2,4,6 – trichloroanisole	Cork with mold sterilized by chloro compounds
Moldy-earthy	2-ethyl-fenchol	Barrels or wood treated with cholorphenol
Vinegar	Acetic acid	Bacteria spoilage or aging in barrels
Leathery-bacon	4-ethyl-phenol	Yeast: Brettanomyces/Dekkera
Horsey-barnyard	4-ethyl-phenol	Yeast: Brettanomyces/Dekkera

It is important to consider that analyzing aromas solely in a scientific manner falls short if we don't consider subjective elements as well. Subjective experiences vary from person to person regarding their own cultural background. Personal experience will shape perception, which will be determined by the specific cultural environment the person grew up in: language, food exposure, religion, values, and so on. In general, wine reviewers create their own analogies expressing in their own way how the wine tastes to them. You will be able to see some examples of this later in the book.

Smell

Scent is the perception provided by our olfactory epithelium and is best explained when we sniff an odorous molecule or fragrance, a mix of odor compounds, from the wine or food. For example, direct olfaction, or direct smelling:

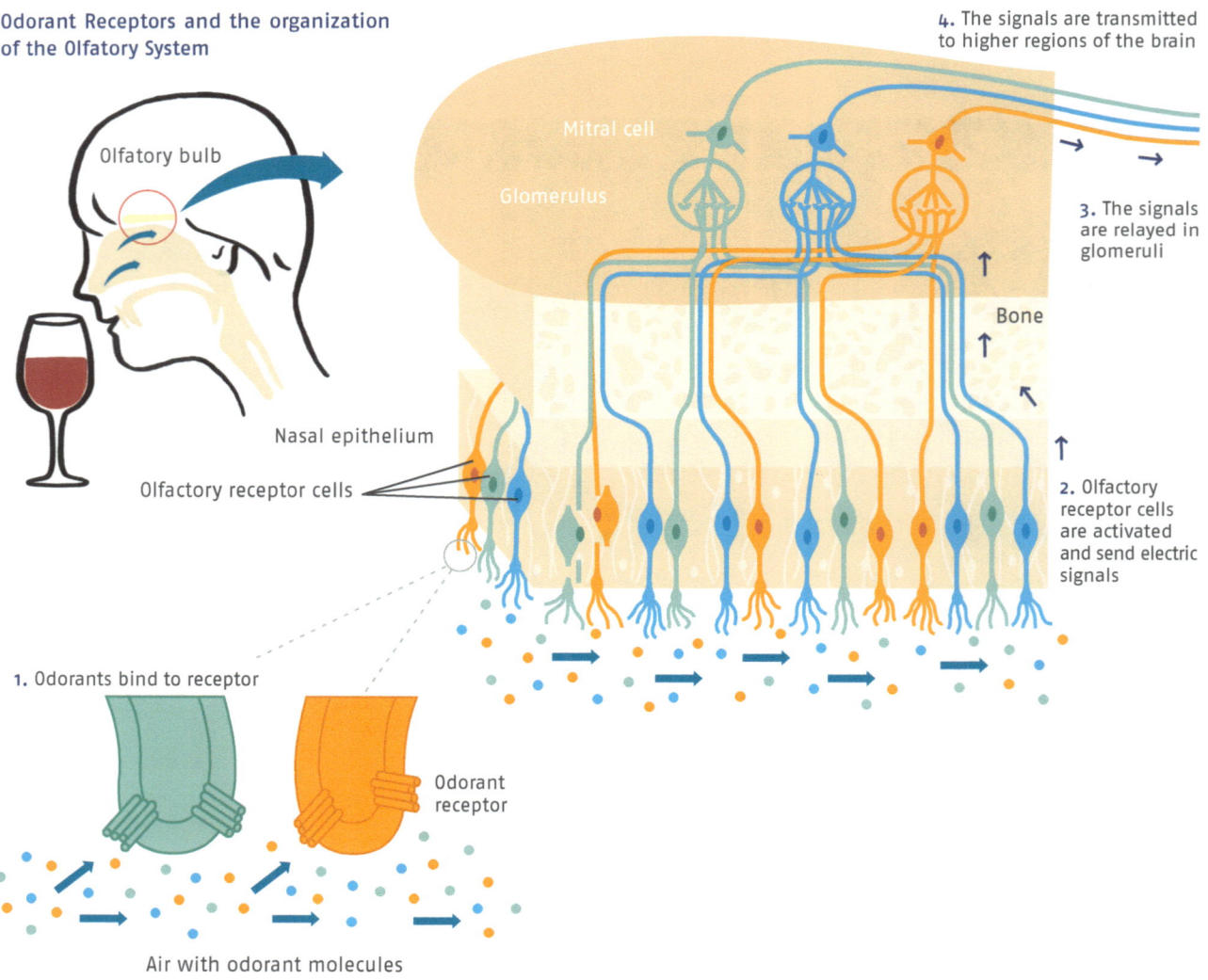

Odorant Receptors and the organization of the Olfatory System

Aroma:

This is the perception given by our olfactory epithelium when the wine or food is in the mouth. An example of this is retronasal olfaction, the practice of sipping wine and pulling air in at the same time. This produces faster oxidation which then produces stronger flavors that the brain is quickly able to identify. Volatile molecules present in the mouth reach the olfactory epithelium retronasally with the air we breathe. If you pinch your nose, you will lose this perception and realize how important it is. You are left with the sense of taste, which includes acidic, sweet, salty, bitter and umami, along with various trigeminal (thermal, mechanical and chemical) sensations. These communicate electronically with our brain to let us know whether something stings or burns, is astringent or refreshing ... how cool is that!

Flavor:

This is the combination of olfactory, gustatory and trigeminal (thermal, mechanical and chemical) sensations perceived during tasting. That is what we commonly call "TASTE."

Thermal Sensations: refers to the temperature sensation of cold and warm.

Mechanical Sensations: refers to the sensation of pain like burning or spicy hot.

Chemical Sensations: Refers to the detection of chemical irritants in the mouth and nose, or on the skin. This sensory system is anatomically independent from the senses of taste and smell.

The word *aroma* also designates the mix of volatile odorant found in food and drinks. So you can use these techniques of "TASTE" for any type of beverage and/or food. Remember, wine tasting is not the only sensorial experience; everything that you eat or drink should be a celebration of the senses.

The Art of Wine Tasting

A lot of people believe tasting wine is the simple action of taking a sip and swallowing immediately. This, however, is not tasting; it is just drinking wine. Tasting, whether food or beverage, is more than just putting something in your mouth and trying to squeeze out a quick flavor. Certainly it is deeper than that, as I mentioned before. Tasting requires the use of and connection to all your senses, like hearing, observing, touching, smelling and tasting.

First, like a yogi you need to clear everything that is blocking your mind. Second, like a Jedi, you need to connect fully with your senses. After that, you are ready to taste.

The force will be with you, my friends.

First of all, you will need a set of good wine glasses, not the ones from the dollar store. Today, you can get decent glassware at a reasonable price at many stores. Good wine deserves a good glass and there are many brands you can choose from.

Let's grab our glass and start filling it up one-third with wine. There are four major steps taken when you taste wine:

1. Observation (sight)

2. Olfaction (nose)

3. Palate (mouth)

4. Conclusion (senses)

So let us begin!

1. Observation (sight):

Observation is a very important step when starting to unveil the age and quality of any wine. Preferably over a white background, angle your glass of wine to observe the wine's color, clarity, brilliance and viscosity. With red wines, the color depth or intensity will give you a clue about the age. For example, they tend to become lighter in color as they age. When young, the most common colors in red wine are pale ruby, ruby, violet, garnet, purple, deep purple and inky black. When aged, red colors begin softening and become brick-red, orange, brown and tawny. White wines usually are opposite ... they begin darkening with age. White wine colors when young are pale straw, straw, green-yellow, pale-yellow, pale-gold, gold (older), deep-gold (old) and brown (very old). Another element we mention is clarity, which means that wines should be brilliant without cloudiness or haziness. If you encounter this, it can signal a flaw in the wine. A clear wine still can have some sediment, whether it is young or old. This is acceptable and is not a fault in the wine. Decanting the wine will remove the sediment. If that is the case, after removing the sediment from your wine, swirl the wine in your glass and observe it run down the sides. If it moves slowly back down, forming the so called "legs" (also known as "tears"), it's likely that the wine has a high level of viscosity (body) as well as a high alcohol content. Usually the higher the alcohol in wine the more full bodied the wine will be.

2. Olfaction (nose):

When the surface of the wine is stationary, you first detect the most volatile and odorous molecules. This initial encounter is magical and often very different from those that follow. At this moment wine will start opening up!

Begin by swirling the wine. This enables other molecules to turn into gas and reach the cavities in your nose. It also oxidizes the components, modifying the molecules and consequently the scents. Describe your perceptions. Wine appreciation is subjective to a certain degree because you are describing what you perceive based on environmental, emotional, and personal experiences in life (your invisible perceptual backpack). Taking it a step farther, where you were born and the type of food you were exposed to growing up will influence your ability to taste wine and food. I remember when I was studying at the Culinary Institute of America, I had a classmate who had a hard time describing berry notes like strawberry, raspberry, and blackberry. For the most part, any type of red wine has a remembrance of berries ... so why was this person unable to detect them? Berries are readily available year-round in California and Chile. This made me think my classmate didn't come from California or Chile, so he didn't grow up eating raspberries, strawberries or blackberries like many of us. He was from India, where berries are not common fruits, so it was difficult for him to name the aromatic nuances that a lot of us identified in wine with these particular fruits. On the other hand, he was great picking up oaky and spicy aromas, which a lot of us were not so good at identifying. My classmate, as I mentioned, was originally from India and Indian cuisine uses a wide varieties of spices (mmm, I love Indian food exactly for that reason ... spices!) but I wasn't exposed to such a rainbow of spice aromatics until I moved to California and experienced different types of cuisine like Indian, Pakistani, Japanese, Korean, Vietnamese ... you name it! The more you smell, the better you'll become at describing aromas in wine. The more open you are to exploring different types of food, the better. So start using your nose, literally and figuratively.

3. Palate (mouth):

The mouth is not only an instrument to mutilate food like in a shark attack movie ... in your mouth you can perceive different types of tastes. Let's see which ones there are.

The most common types of tastes we know in Western culture are sweet, sour, bitter, umami, and salty. There is no salt in wine, so we will focus on the other tastes in addition to acidic and tannic.

Retro-Olfaction Technique

Describing aromas on the palate, (retro-olfaction):

Take a sip of wine and hold it in your mouth. Wine warms up in the mouth and molecules that could not make the transition to volatility are now able to do so. Professional wine tasters intensify the new sensations by inhaling a breath of air and circulating it through the wine. Retronasal olfaction allows for the observation of intensely persistent aromas. The duration of these aromas and the aftertaste is one criterion for assessing wine quality. The longer the flavor remains in your mouth the more complex the wine will be. The flavor that remains should be delicious, harmonious, well balanced, and pleasant. If that is not the case, and the aftertaste is unpleasant, hot, too acidic, too tannic, or dies right away after you swallow the wine, then you are not experiencing a very good

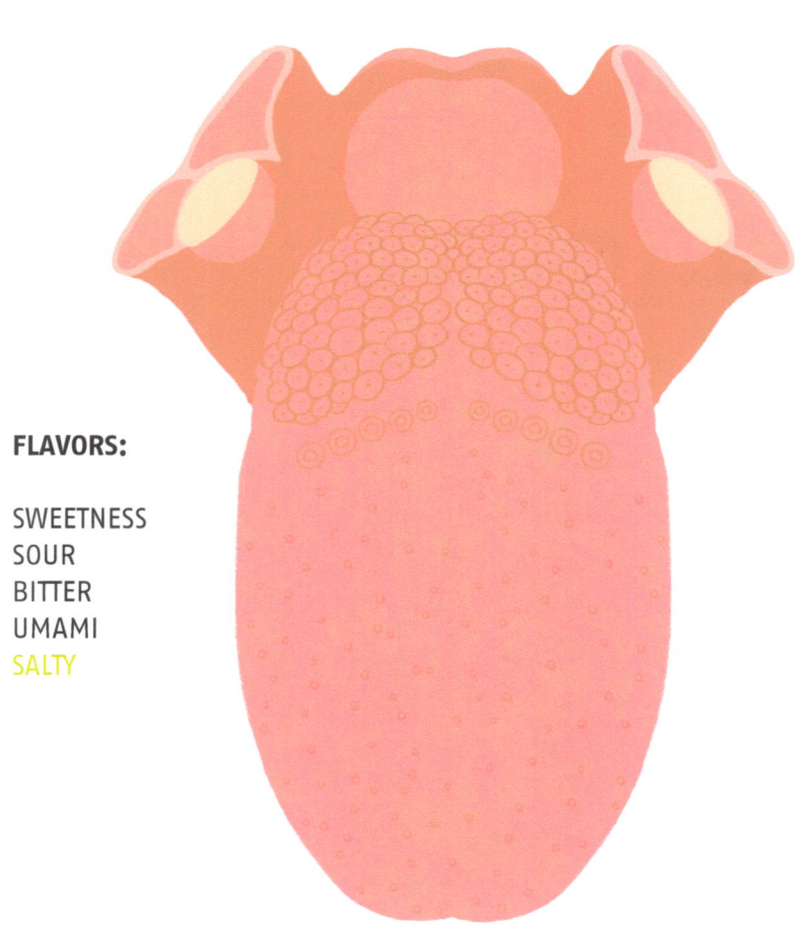

FLAVORS:

SWEETNESS
SOUR
BITTER
UMAMI
SALTY

wine. The wine may need aging because the finish needs to be smooth and persistent. Like Bruce Willis in the Die Hard movies, wine seems as if it is going to die but remains alive over and over, persistently. Wine has a purpose and that purpose is to provide pleasure, like a smooth caress on your senses. Got it!

Let´s describe them!

Bitterness: It is usually created by high alcohol and high tannins. Usually tasted on the back of your tongue when the tannin is coming from the oak, and in the front of the mouth when the tannin is coming from the fruit.

Sweetness: Occurs only in wines that have some residual sugar left over after fermentation, common in some table (dry) wines, and can be found in sweet, dessert and fortified wines.

Sour: Sour, sometimes called "tart," indicates the acidity in wine. White wines and some lighter-style red wines contain a higher degree of acidity, like Pinot Noir, Chablis or Sauvignon Blanc, and perhaps Champagne and some sparkling wines. Acidity is fundamental for the vibrancy and crispiness of a wine and is also a key element for the longevity of any wine.

Tannin: Tannin frequently exists in red wine and is less common in white wine. There are two sources of tannins: the fruit (stems, seeds, and skin), and the barrel. Regarding tannins that are derived from the fruit, when the wine is too young, they can dry out the palate excessively and are very noticeable. Tannins coming from the barrel give a bitter sensation in the back of the throat as opposed to tannins that come from the fruit, which create a sensation at the front of the mouth. If there are a lot of tannins in the wine, it can actually coat the whole mouth, blocking the fruit flavors. Tannin is not a taste, it is a tactile sensation. If you really want to have a direct experience with tannins, go to the farmers market, buy grapes with seeds, and chew the seeds and stems. The rough sensation in the mouth that remains after chewing the seeds and stems is a result of the tannins. Tannins are present in other beverages as well. Black and green teas contain strong tannic notes if they are robustly brewed. Most common tannic red wines are Tannat, Cabernet Sauvignon, Barolos, Barbarescos and Petit Syrah, to name a few.

Umami: Also called MSG, it is savory and also described as a meaty taste imparted by glutamate and ribonucleotides. This savory taste occurs naturally in many foods including meat, fish, vegetables and dairy products. Sometimes we describe wine using the term "meaty" and to a certain extent some wines have umami flavor nuances. Generally, this flavor is very subtle and makes me think of soy sauce. If you have experienced the same type of taste, now you know where it is coming from!
*To learn more about umami check the wine and food section.

4. Conclusion, (senses):

In this final step, we decide if the wine we are experiencing is awesome, mediocre or something in between. It is important to take in consideration several factors in this stage, for example:

• If the wine is coming from a cool or warm weather condition.

• If this wine is a single grape variety or is a blend.

• If the wine is a good representation of the appellation, country, region or sub-region where it come from.

• The price of the wine is not necessarily a good indicator in evaluating the quality of a wine, since we find wine in the U.S. from different local regions and from all over the world. Prices are contingent upon numerous factors such as economy, taxation, trade agreements, cost of labor, cost of land, type of production, quantity of production, etc. These and other elements are going to have an impact on the price of your wine on the shelf of your local store.

In my opinion, probably the most important tool and form of evaluation of quality belongs to you and is free. Your senses! With your senses you'll be able to evaluate the intensity and complexity of the aromas and flavors when you smell the wine. The length of the finish should always be enjoyable, smooth and seductive, like a caress on your palate that persist for a while or perhaps, using another analogy... like a seductive kiss that can take you away from planet Earth in just a sip. For me, a really good wine should make you smile.

Salud!

Common Aromas

White Wines and Champagne:

Citric Notes:
Lemon, Grapefruit, Orange, Lime, Lemon Zest

Tropical Notes:
Pineapple, Banana, Mango, Guava, Melon

Stone Fruit Notes:
Peach, Nectarine, Apricot, Apple, Pear

Floral Notes:
Honey, White Rose, Violet, Orange Blossom

Herbaceous and Vegetal Notes:
Green Grass, Jalapeño pepper, Green Olives

Exotic Notes:
Lychee, Muscat, Quince, Kiwi, Yeast

Roasted Notes:
Roasted Almond, Roasted Hazelnut, Caramel

Animal Notes:
Butter, Cream, Sweaty, Cat Pee

Red Wines:

Berry Notes:
Blackberry, Blueberry, Strawberry, Raspberry, Red Currant, Black Currant

Stone Notes:
Black Cherry, Red Cherry, Plum, Prune

Floral Notes:
Acacia, Linden, Honey, Rose, Violet, Orange Blossom

Vegetal & Earthy Notes:
Green Pepper, Green Grass, Eucalyptus, Mint, Cut Hay
Green Tea, Black Tea, Mushroom, Truffle

Spicy Notes:
Cedar, Pine, Licorice, Black Currant, Boxwood, Thyme, Vanilla, Cinnamon, Clove, Pepper, Saffron, Tobacco

Exotic Notes:
Bacon, Yeast

Roasted Notes:
Toast, Roasted Almond, Roasted Hazelnut, Caramel
Coffee, Dark Chocolate, Smoke, Roasted Walnut

Animal notes:
Butter, Leather, Musk, Barnyard

Tasting wine as an objective practice...really?

Lately, there has been a lot of controversy in the wine world regarding the use of a scoring system for wine evaluation rather than using a direct opinion. I would like to analyze the subject and in that analysis, you will find my personal opinion and thoughts.

I'm not sure exactly when the scoring system began in the U.S. and what exactly the main purpose for it was, but I can assume the scoring system was likely born as a means of helping and guiding new wine enthusiasts and consumers. Additionally, I assume it was designed to make wine more accessible, given that there is an overwhelming amount of it in the market and a skyrocketing increase in the number of wineries, subsequently producing a large selection in varieties, which have steadily increased from the late 80s and 90s until today. California alone has more than 3,600 wineries! This increase is not only unique to California; all over the U.S. there are more than 8,000 wineries. This does not take into account the availability of imported wines from all over the world. I think these are all fair considerations when contemplating the origins of the scoring system, don't you?

After awhile, when an individual or some media source gains credibility, people have a tendency to develop a comfort zone, which delegates the responsibility of selection to an external source. These external sources influence a large number of people, and in the case of wine, it influences the type and style of wine consumers buy. I believe a lot of people enjoy convenience, so this easily became the norm and almost an established method of wine selection for the common consumer. Due to this established scoring system, the buying practices of restaurants and retailers have also been strongly influenced because certain wines became a "hot commodity," easy to buy and easy to sell when their score is high.

As for wineries, they focus heavily on aligning taste to the particular scoring system/media outlet to ensure their wines will be awarded a good score. After all, a good score equals good sales and an increase in price. Lastly, a good score means recognition. However, under that premise the industry forgot some important fundamentals of wine ... such as diversity in style, typicity, the *terroir*, and the personality of the wine. These attributes all took a back seat to generic styles of wine produced with the main purpose of pleasing the media and, subsequently, consumers who follow that trend. It has been forgotten that TASTE is for the most part a subjective practice. When the scoring system was born, something that is subjective quickly became objective. I will argue that a scenario can exist called "objectivlty."

Objectivity-in-Parenthesis

Taste for the most part is a subjective practice, as I mentioned before, but there is also a degree of "objectivity-in-parenthesis" as well. What is that? As the biologist Humberto Maturana suggests, "the notion of reality" can't be separated from the observer but can be extracted and explained in the domain of language, not necessarily in the domain of reality as a reality existing independently (objectively) from the person who describes a particular phenomenon or object. Many variables exist that need to be considered, and as Maturana described, human beings have an invisible backpack of experiences we carry with us, even before we are born. In this invisible backpack we accumulate experiences during our lifetime, and the historical accumulation of experiences is derived from such diverse sources as family (values, morals, emotions, etc.), or from the environment (language, social norms, religion, laws, TV, entertainment, etc.). Maturana claims all of these, including our own biology, contributes to the shaping of our view of the world (which we think is independent from us), and what we call "external reality," or objectivity is in reality, objectively. This makes me remember the experience I mentioned before with my classmate from India and how good he was at describing spices. He grew up in an environment (domain) where he was exposed to a vast variety of spices, but he struggled with describing berries because these were not in his environment. So, in his domain of reality (objectivity), berries did not exist and because of this, his objective conclusion is based on familial and environmental factors based on where and how he was living (objectively).

Let's take a look at a graphic example comparing objectivity and objectively. Below are two wine descriptions and their respective scores from two well known wine magazines in the U.S. It is important to note two different representatives from two different wine magazines did this tasting and both tasted the exact same wine.

Quinetessa 2007

Tasting notes by a representative from magazine one
Cabernet Sauvignon, 2007
Score: 95 points

"A very fine Cab from the estate, which is in the North-central part of the Rutherford appellation ... the flavors are extraordinary. They flood the mouth with the essence of Cabernet, with ripe blackberries, black currants, raspberries and mocha, and the spicy finish lasts for a full minute. Should provide great drinking through 2019 at least."

Tasting notes by a representative from magazine two
Cabernet Sauvignon, 2007
Score: 91 points

"Dark ruby/purple, with sweet black currant, cherry, and loamy soil notes intermixed with some subtle spice box and background oak, this wine is rich and medium to full-bodied, with round, silky tannins, and an attractive set of aromatics. Very accessible and drinkable now, it should age nicely for 15 or more years."

Now, if you carefully notice the narrative, both tasters only agree on one flavor, "black currant." Everything else was a result of their personal and individual narrative, in other words, subjectivity. Even the score for both wines is different, (objectively). So scoring a wine cannot be a purely objective practice, and there are hundreds of thousands of descriptions like these which prove the point that objective practices are sometimes "objectivity-in-parenthesis" views and can't be considered universal.

So what is a consumer to do?

Follow your own path. Explore and enjoy wine as a practice of pleasure, not a number. A number cannot measure an emotional experience or quality. Trust your TASTE, be open-minded as well as an explorer. If you want to deepen your knowledge in wine, take a class, read, or interact with people who can give guidance. Enjoy the vast and diverse universe of wine available to you. My invitation is to connect with your senses; that's the secret, if there is one. Feel them and start unfolding and creating your own experiences and at the end of the day, you should be the person who judges the wine because you are the one who is having the direct experience with it.

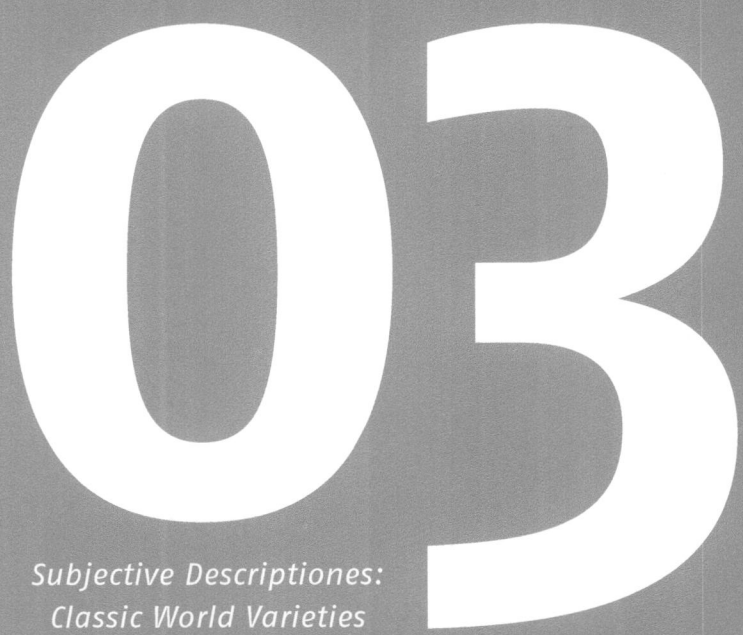

Subjective Descriptiones:
Classic World Varieties

The idea of this chapter is **to motivate** you to explore different grape varieties. Exploring different styles of wine and being open-minded is very important in order to grow an appreciation of this amazing beverage. Here in California, I encounter many amazingly different styles of wine and also some interesting varieties besides the traditional ones that many winemakers are experimenting with, for example, interesting varieties like Grenache, Tannat, Negrette, Teroldego, Barolo, Malbec, as well as some other interesting and exciting blends. We are so lucky here in the U.S. because of the variety of wines from different regions, both nationally and internationally. This is not very common in other countries, so it is a real privilege. I want to encourage you to take advantage of these amazing opportunities to explore, taste, and learn more about wine. This chapter is a description of grape varieties considered to be world-wide classics, with the exception of Cabernet Franc, Malbec and Carménère. The descriptions are very general and will give you **a good frame of reference** when it comes to particular varieties and which countries produce them.

Chardonnay

The Queen, or in more informal terms, the Lady Gaga of white wine varietals is cultivated from Burgundy, France, to Chile and Australia. Chardonnay is arguably the most popular white wine in California and the world. Common flavors include green apple, pear, citrus and tropical fruit. Chardonnay is produced in a wide variety of styles depending on the type of climate and soil. Wines from cooler climatic areas tend to be lighter-bodied and have a high acidity, with flavors leaning towards tart green apple, tropical fruit (pineapple, papaya and mango), with pronounced citrus notes. Warmer climate Chardonnays tend to be fuller-bodied with aromatics of ripe apple, pear, honey, and even peach. Malolactic fermentation (conversion of malic acid into lactic acid) adds buttery flavors and a creamier texture, while barrel fermentation and oak aging add complexity, tertiary aromas, and flavors of toast, honey, vanilla and spices. In terms of family, Chardonnay's parents are Pinot and Gouais Blanc.

Chardonnay is Cultivated in the Following Countries

- **France:** Burgundy, Champagne, and parts of the Languedoc-Roussillon

- **United States:** California, Washington State, Oregon, New York State, Virginia

- Chile
- Italy
- Spain
- Portugal
- UK
- Germany
- Bulgaria
- Romania
- Hungary
- Slovenia
- Croatia
- New Zealand
- South Africa
- Australia
- Argentina

Sauvignon Blanc

In California, this is probably the most popular white grape varietal after Chardonnay. Most Sauvignon Blancs fall into two of three distinct styles: those modeled after the wines of Sancerre and Pouilly Fume from France's Loire Valley and those modeled after the Bordeaux region. I think it is also fair to say there is a third category, the New Zealand style, which is more grassy and citrusy in character than the Loire Valley Sauvignon Blanc. Wines made in the Loire style tend to be lean, displaying citrus flavors and minerals with great acidity. Although it is uncommon, oak aging is sometimes found in wines of this style; the Fume Blanc from Mondavi was a great example. The other major style of Sauvignon Blanc is modeled after the white Bordeaux. These wines are commonly a Sémillon-Sauvignon Blanc blend and tend to be fuller-bodied, with flavors of melon, fig, smoke and spices that remind me more of a California style than their counterparts from Sancere, New Zealand, South Africa and Chile. In terms of family, Sauvignon Blanc's only known parent is Savagnin. Another interesting fact is that Sauvignon Blanc is a sibling of Chenin Blanc and Trousseau. Also, Sauvignon Blanc is a half sibling of Gruner Veltliner, Silvaner and Verdelho, to name a few.

Sauvignon Blanc is Cultivated in the Following Countries

- **France:** Loire Valley, Bordeaux

- **United States:** California, Washington States

- Chile
- Italy
- Spain
- Portugal
- Germany
- Austria
- Romania
- Republic of Moldova
- Russia
- Ukraine
- Australia
- Switzerland
- Czech Republic
- New Zealand
- South Africa

Sémillon

This varietal is cultivated only in the Sauternes region of Bordeaux in south-west France, which is considered Sémillon's birthplace. Sémillon in the Bordeaux region usually is blended with Sauvignon Blanc to produce the famous delicious, late harvest, botrytis (grape) dessert wine Sauternes. The flavor profile of Sémillon sometimes depends on where it is growing (cold or warm climate), and can be similar to the herbaceous type of Sauvignon Blanc. Here in California, fully ripe Sémillon is fuller-bodied and has more viscosity and stone fruit character (think about Paso Robles, for instance) compared to Sauvignon Blanc from Bordeaux. In terms of family, the parents still remain unknown.

Semillon is Cultivated in the Following Countries:

- **France:** Bourdeaux
- **United States:** California
- **Chile**
- **Canada:** British Columbia
- New Zealand
- South Africa
- Argentina
- Australia
- Uruguay
- Portugal
- Hungary
- Turkey
- Russia
- Cyprus
- Greece
- Israel

Riesling

Though Riesling grapes are considered one of the world's greatest white wines, it sometimes doesn't get the respect it deserves, despite the fact that Riesling is made in a wider range of styles than any other single grape varietal. It can range from bone dry sparkling wine to some of the most sublime dessert wines produced anywhere, with everything in between. Not to mention that Riesling has one of the best aging capabilities compared to other white wines. The range of flavors found in Riesling is also remarkable and can remind you of aromatic nuances of green apple, lemon-lime citrus, tropical fruit, stone fruits like peaches and apricots, and slate minerals (particularly the German ones from Mosel). When infected with botrytis, Riesling can be made into a luscious and complex dessert wine, yum! It is also important to consider the German Riesling. Top quality categories are found in the QMP (Qualitätswein mit Prädikat), and there are several styles in this category: QMP that range from dryer to sweeter (Kabinett, Spätlese, Auslese, Beerenauslese, Eiswine/Icewine and Trockenbeerenauslese). In terms of family, Riesling's parent, according to DNA, is Gouais Blanc. Gouais Blanc also has parent-offspring with at least eighty other grape varieties (very active parent!). Surprisingly, Riesling is related with other many well known grape varieties like Chardonnay, Gamay Noir and Furmint, to name just a few.

Riesling is Cultivated in the Following Countries:

- **Germany:** Rheingau, Rheinhessen, Rhein, Pfalz, Mozel
- **France:** Alsace
- **United States:** Washington State, New York State, California
- Chile
- Canada
- Italy
- Spain
- Austria
- Hungary
- New Zealand
- South Africa
- Australia
- China

Cabernet Sauvignon

Ranked first among the noble red varietals because it produces an enormous range and number of complex and profound wines in so many wine regions throughout the world, Cabernet Sauvignon is really the rock star of the red wines. If I have to make an analogy with a rocker, I would say that Cabernet is like an amalgamation of Elvis Presley and Bob Dylan, because when aged it can be magnificent like Elvis, but as I said before, it can also be profound like Dylan. One can find Cabernet-based wines in many areas of France, Eastern Europe, Italy, Chile, Australia and various regions of the United States; best known is Napa Valley. Flavors commonly found in Cabernet include blackberries, black cherry, tertiary aromas like cassis, chocolate, cocoa, coffee, mint, herbs, cedar and oak-aging, plus nuances of vanilla and other spices. In its youth, Cabernet Sauvignon is dark, concentrated and tannic, sometimes requiring ten to fifteen years of aging to soften, especially the ones from Bordeaux and some from Napa Valley. In France, Cabernet Sauvignon is often blended with other varietals, (especially Merlot and Cabernet Franc) to soften its tannins and give more complexity to the wine. In terms of family, Cabernet Sauvignon's parents are Cabernet Franc and Sauvignon Blanc.

Cabernet Sauvignon is Cultivated in the Following Countries:

- **France:** Bordeaux and part of the Lanquedoc-Roussillon.
- **United States:** California, Washington State
- **Chile:** Maipo, Colchagua Valley
- Italy
- Spain
- Portugal
- Bulgaria
- Greece
- Ukraine
- Russia
- Turkey
- Romania
- Slovenia
- Croatia
- Argentina
- Australia
- Mexico
- Canada
- New Zealand
- South Africa
- China
- Japan

Cabernet Franc

Likely one of the most ancient and more important varieties in Bordeaux, recent studies show that Cabernet Franc's origin is Spanish País Vasco, the Basque region. Cabernet Franc is similar in structure and flavor to Cabernet Sauvignon, but not quite as full bodied, and less tannic and acidic. This variety can have great aroma and herbaceous character. In Bordeaux, Cabernet Franc is most often blended with Merlot and Cabernet Sauvignon. In the Loire Valley, it is usually made as a single grape variety and the result is superb. In terms of family, Cabernet Franc's parents are Morenoa and Hondarribi Beltza.

Cabernet Franc is Cultivated in the Following Countries:

- **France:** Loire Valley, Bordeaux, southwest France
- **United States:** California, Oregon, Washington State, Michigan, Virginia, New York State
- Chile
- Italy
- Spain
- Portugal
- Romania
- Hungary
- Greece
- Cyprus
- Israel
- Canada
- Uruguay
- Argentina
- Australia
- New Zealand
- South Africa
- China

Merlot

This variety is widely planted, particularly in the Pomerol and Languedoc regions of Bordeaux, France. Most consumers in the U.S. probably don't know that Merlot is the single most planted grape variety in France (and probably in the world). After the popularity of the movie Sideways, Merlot suffered a deep decline in sales and the reputation went downhill in the U.S. However, Merlot produces extraordinary grapes that usually ripen earlier then Cabernet Sauvignon and wines that have softer and more velvety tannins then Cabernet. This makes Merlot more fruity and easy to drink, especially at a young age. Probably one of the most well known in popularity and price is Chateau Petrus from Pomerol, a very expensive wine made 100% with Merlot grapes. In terms of family, Merlot's parents are Cabernet Franc and Magdaleine Noire des Charentes.

Merlot is Cultivated in the Following Countries:

- **France:** Bordeaux and part of the Lanquedoc-Roussillon
- **United States:** California, Washington State, New York State
- Chile
- Australia
- Canada
- Mexico
- Turkey
- Greece
- Uruguay
- Brazil
- China
- Japan
- India

Pinot Noir

In contrast with the fate suffered by Merlot after the movie *Sideways*, Pinot Noir's popularity grew enormously in the U.S. In my opinion, this grape variety is great so I'm glad the perception of it was positively affected, although I wasn't happy about the rise in price! Pinot Noir is relatively soft, fruity, and easy to enjoy. It is also known for its lush, silky texture. Pinot Noir has flavors that include red cherry, raspberry, strawberry, tea, cola, spices and earth. With bottle aging, flavors of game, truffles, exotic spices and mineral complexities evolve. The real origin of Pinot Noir is still unknown, but Burgundy is probably where Pinot Noir grows best and produces magnificently. There are around 1,000 different clones of this variety. If you see the numbers 113, 114, 115, 667, 777 and 828 on some bottles in California, or if you hear winemakers in tasting rooms or in the winery talking about these numbers, they are referring to the most common clones used in the U.S. for Pinot Noirs. Other clones also commonly used are Pommard (UCD4 and 5), Wadenswil (UCD1) and Mariafeld (UCD 23). Pinot's history dates back approximately 2,000 years and, as I mentioned earlier, Pinot Noir is a mutation of Pinot as they are: Pinot Gris, Pinot Blanc and Pinot Meunier. It is likely these are the most common clonal mutations of Pinot that you are familiar with. Is also likely that Pinot is a great-grandparent of Syrah.

Pinot Noir is Cultivated in the Following Countries:

- **France:** Burgundy, the Loir Valley, Jura
- **United States:** California, Oregon
- Chile
- Italy
- Austria
- Germany
- Switzerland
- New Zealand
- South Africa
- Australia
- Argentina
- Romania
- Hungary

Syrah

Grown in many of the world's great wine regions, arguably the greatest examples of Syrah are found in the tiny northern Rhone Valley communities of Cote Rotie and Hermitage. There, the grapes are grown on incredibly steep slopes and yields wines of remarkable power, depth and complexity. Syrah is also a major blending component of many southern Rhone blends such as Chateauneauf-du-Pape. Australia produces world-class Syrahs, (labeled Shiraz) from regions including New South Wales and South Australia. Syrah is made in a wide range of styles, from light nouveau-style wines all the way to tannic, inky monsters, with every stop in between. Syrah is also successfully cultivated in California and Washington State. Common flavors for Syrah include blackberry, black raspberry, floral, leather, mineral, earth, game, herb and pepper. In terms of family, Syrah's parents are Mondeuse Blanche and Dureza.

Syrah is Cultivated in the following Countries:

- **France:** Northern and Southern Rhone Valleys and parts of the Midi

- **United States:** California, Washington State, Oregon, Idaho, Arizona, Texas, Colorado

- Chile
- Italy
- Spain
- Portugal
- South Africa
- Australia
- Argentina

Carménère

Carménère is the prodigal son of Bordeaux, originally from France. It was widely cultivated in Medoc in southwest France in the early 1800s. After the *phylloxera* pest infestation in the 1870s, this variety almost completely disappeared from France. The first Carménère vines were brought to Chile in the mid-nineteenth century as Merlot. In 1994 ampelographer J-M Boursiquot identified the "Chilean Merlot" as Carménère, which was confirm by DNA analysis in 1997. After that discovery, Chileans have been improving and converting Carménère in an exciting variety of wines to explore. Carménère when in full maturity can have notes of black fruit like blackberries and blueberries, with overtones of coffee and chocolate. When it is not very mature, Carménère can have herbaceous flavors like grass and hay. In terms of Carménère's family, parents are Cabernet Franc and Gros Cabernet.

Carménère is Cultivated in the following Countries:

- **France:** Bordeaux (Cahors)

- **Chile:** Limarí, Aconcagua, Maipo, Cachapoal, Colchagua, Curico

- Italy
- Argentina
- China

Malbec

In native southwest France, Malbec is also known as Cot. The name Cot derives from a contraction of Cahors in Quercy. From Quercy, this variety was introduced to the Gironde in the 1800s, and you can still find some of these grapes in the region of Cahors and southern France. Malbec, or Cot, is one of the five main red varietals from Bordeaux. The others are: Merlot, Cabernet Sauvignon, Cabernet Franc and Petit Verdot. A French agronomist, Michel Pouget, introduced Malbec to Argentina. Michel brought Malbec and other cuttings to Mendoza from France in 1868. This later was propagated throughout the province of Mendoza by other new immigrants from Italy and Spain. Most of the Malbec today is concentrated in Mendoza (85%), but you will also find Malbec in Lujan de Cuyo, Uco Valley (Tunuyán, San Carlos), Patagonia, (Neuquen and Rio Negro), and in the north, Salta and Catamarca. Malbec has an intense purple color with flavors of black fruits like blueberry, plum and blackberry. Some have gamey and violet notes. Malbec has a range of styles from soft and fruity to more strong, structured, elegant and age-worthy.

Malbec is Cultivated in the following countries:

- **France:** Bordeaux (Cahors)

- **Argentina:** Salta, Catamarca, Lujan de Cuyo, Uco , Patagonia

- Chile

- **United States:** California, Washington State

- Italy
- Australia
- New Zealand

This is a very small selection of grapes, keeping in mind there are approximately 10,000 different grape varieties around the world. If you would like to learn more about them, I recommend the book by Jancis Robinson, Julia Harding and Jose Vouillamoz,Wine Grapes. Within this book, you will find information about more than 1,368 different varieties and their origin.

04
Tools for Serving Wine

Chapter 4 is a fun chapter. Here you will find tips about what you need to know in order to enjoy your favorite wine in a better way. Also if you are planning a trip to any wine region, you can learn the unwritten etiquette of **visiting tasting rooms.**

Important tools and considerations in wine

Today, an amazing variety of wine gadgets exist and like everybody else, certainly I enjoy the new advancements in technology. I do, however, tend to be a minimalist and enjoy more simplistic tools rather than the high tech ones. Let's take a look at some basic fundamentals so you may enjoy your wine in the proper and best way.

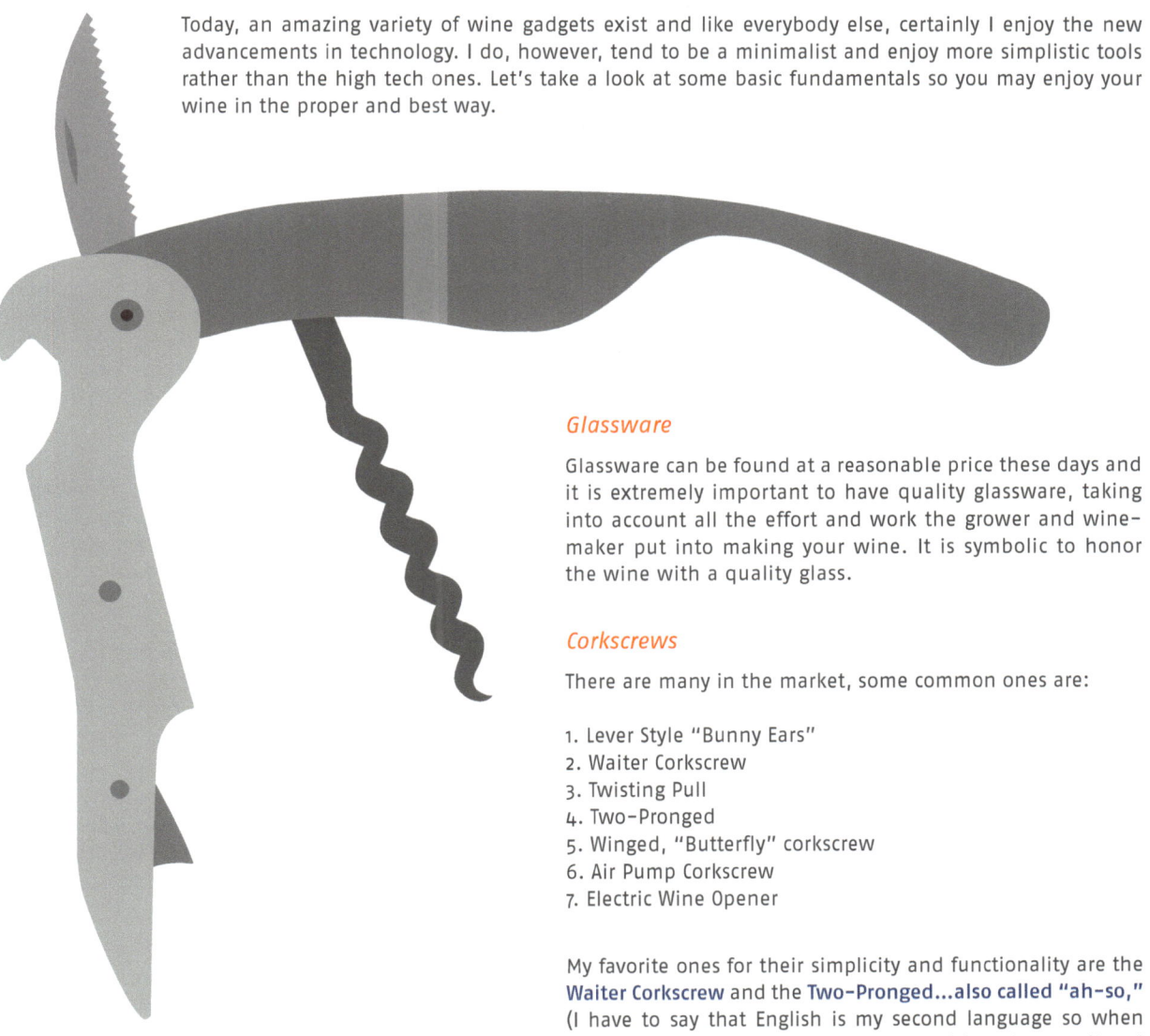

Glassware

Glassware can be found at a reasonable price these days and it is extremely important to have quality glassware, taking into account all the effort and work the grower and winemaker put into making your wine. It is symbolic to honor the wine with a quality glass.

Corkscrews

There are many in the market, some common ones are:

1. Lever Style "Bunny Ears"
2. Waiter Corkscrew
3. Twisting Pull
4. Two-Pronged
5. Winged, "Butterfly" corkscrew
6. Air Pump Corkscrew
7. Electric Wine Opener

My favorite ones for their simplicity and functionality are the **Waiter Corkscrew** and the **Two-Pronged...also called "ah-so,"** (I have to say that English is my second language so when I pronounce that word it doesn't sound how I mean it ... I didn't say asshole!). These two are the ones you really need.

The **Waiter Corkscrew** should be used with bottles when closure is done with natural or synthetic cork and with bottles of wine that haven't been aged for a long time. If you have bottles with cork but they're old, you should use the **ah-so** (glad you can't hear me!), because with time the cork becomes softer due to the prolonged contact with the wine. The **ah-so** is the perfect tool to use in bottles that have been age for a long time (10+years).

Decanters

Decanting is necessary for two basic yet fundamental reasons:

- To remove wine from the sediment which has formed in the bottle.
- To allow the wine to take in oxygen ... *to breathe.*

In the case of older wines, especially reds, with increasing age, many natural deposits of tannins and color pigments settle or collect in the base of the bottle. Both red and white wines, particularly white, can also shed a crystalline deposit due to a precipitation of tartrates. Although all these deposits are harmless, their appearance is distracting and decanting is an easy way to remove the deposits.

Preparing the Bottle and Pouring the Wine

Several hours prior to decanting, move the bottle into an upright position (this counts for older bottles as well as unfiltered young wines). Doing so allows the sediment lying along the side of the bottle to fall to the bottom. Cut away the top quarter inch or so of the foil capsule. This could well reveal a penicillin growth or, if the wine is an old vintage, a fine black deposit. Neither have had contact with the wine, but to avoid any unintentional contamination when removing the cork, it is wise to wipe the lip of the bottle neck and the top of the cork with a clean, damp cloth. Insert a corkscrew and gently withdraw the cork. Place a clean finger inside the top of the bottle and carefully remove any pieces of cork or any tartrate crystals adhering to the inside of the neck, then wipe the lip of the bottle neck with a clean, dry cloth.

Lift the bottle slowly in one hand and the decanter in the other and bring them together over a light source, such as a candle or small lighter, which will reveal any sediment as the wine is poured. (This not only makes you look cool, it is also romantic.) Aim to pour the wine in a slow, steady flow so that the bottle does not jerk and wine does not "gulp for air." Such mishaps will disturb the sediment, and that is not a good thing.

Allowing Wine to Breathe

As soon as you open a bottle of wine, it will be "breathing" but because the surface is very small, the effects of oxygenation are not as intense compared to when you transfer the wine to a decanter, which exposes the wine to air. It is during the decanting process where slow oxidation occurs, and this enables various elements and compounds to form or change in the complex chemical process known as maturation (fast aging). Allowing a wine to breathe is, in effect, creating a rapid maturation. Allowing the wine to breathe also improves young, full-bodied and tannic red wines, making them more soft and smooth.

Storing Wine

According to some studies, 90% of wine in the United States is consumed twenty-four hours after purchase. If you buy a wine that you are planning on drinking next year, it should be kept relatively cool and out of touch with any light source. A dark closet or a cool garage with little or no fluctuation in temperature is a good place. Wines you want to age or cellar for more than a year will need more attention. Avoid drastic fluctuations of temperature. The ideal temperature for the wine to be cellared at is a constant flux of 60–63°F.

Humidity

Humidity helps keep the cork moist. If the cork dries out from lack of moisture, it actually shrinks, which allows oxygen in, permeating the wine. Then, acetobacter kicks in, which oxidizes the wine. The result will be a wine that tastes like vinegar.

Duration

Not all wines need to be aged or cellared. In fact, most wine is consumed young or relatively soon after it is produced, as I mention before. In addition to 90% of all wines being consumed within twenty-four hours of purchase, 90% of wines are meant to be consumed within one year. Some wines will become better over time, while others will not.

Temperature of Serving Wine

It is very important to serve wine at an appropriate temperature because you can then enjoy the wine much more if you are drinking it at the right temperature. When temperature has been carefully considered, the wine is able to express its full range of aromatics. Yum!

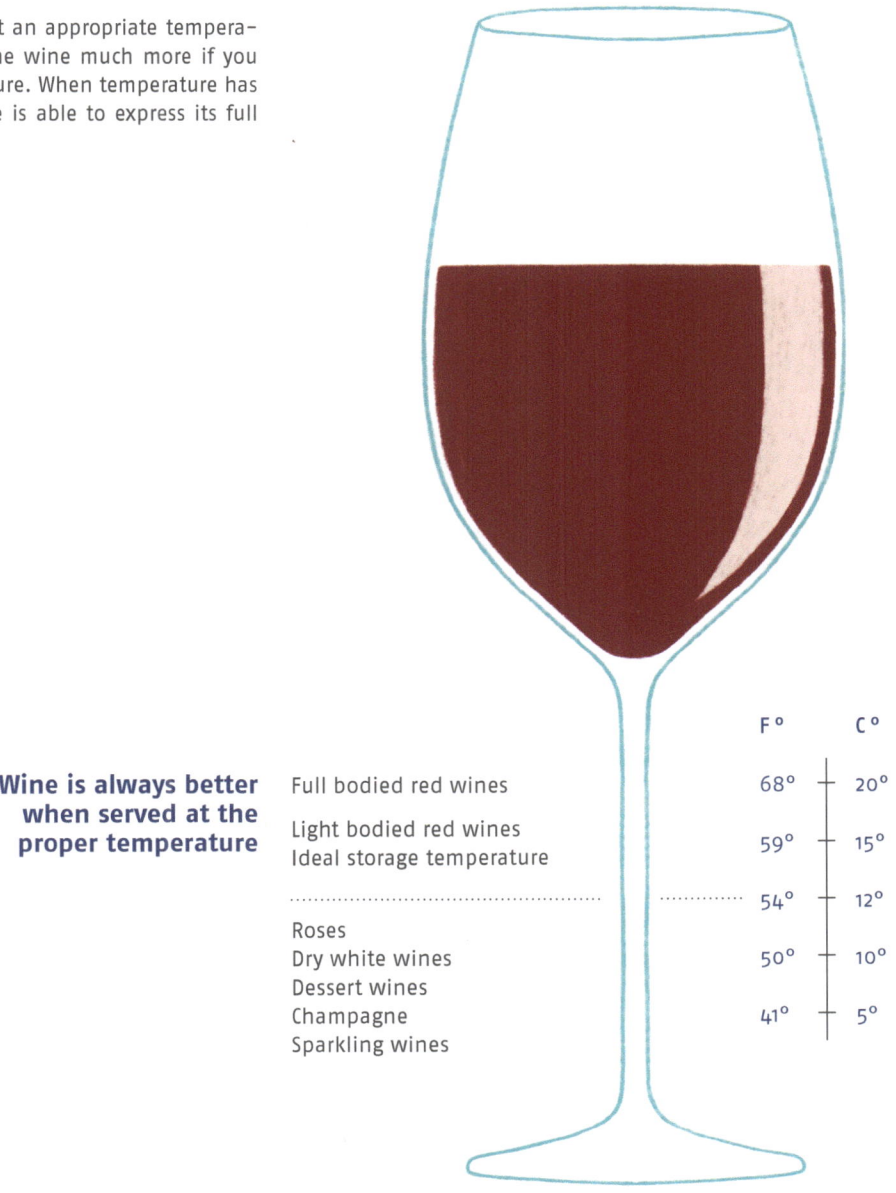

Wine is always better when served at the proper temperature

	F°	C°
Full bodied red wines	68°	20°
Light bodied red wines	59°	15°
Ideal storage temperature		
	54°	12°
Roses		
Dry white wines	50°	10°
Dessert wines		
Champagne	41°	5°
Sparkling wines		

Tasting Room Etiquette

The following are some helpful tips when visiting tasting rooms:

a. **Research** – Be educated about the regions and wineries you are planning on visiting, so you'll know ahead of time what type of wines for which this particular region is well known. If you are planning on staying a few days, most regions here in California are organized and have passports, tours and special discounts for groups and individuals. Also, not all wineries have a tasting room so you may need to schedule an appointment before visiting them.

b. **Attire** - Wear comfortable clothing. I recommend that you don't wear any strong scents, perfume or cologne, when you are tasting. These scents will interfere with your senses and distort the full essence of the wines you will taste. Cologne and perfumes will also interfere with the senses of those around you. So be aware of your personal aroma before going wine tasting, and don't go for a run directly before visiting a tasting room!

c. **Have Your I.D.** – Always bring your I.D., just in case. Especially if you have a baby face, which I think is not a bad thing! I like it when they ask for my I.D.

d. **Be Mindful** - Call ahead if you have a large group and arrive early, if possible, so the wine associate can spend more time with the group answering questions about the winery, particular wines, club membership, etc. Also be respectful with the hours of operation. Sometimes people show up five minutes before closing and stay forty-five minutes to an hour. It is a general rule of thumb to make a purchase if you are staying past hours of operation. Not all tasting room associates will stay open late (past their shift), but for those who do, at least purchase a bottle and leave a tip. That is the polite way of saying thank you.

e. **Don't Overdo It** – If you start early in the morning visiting tasting rooms, I suggest doing two nice and relaxed tastings in the morning and one or two nice tastings in the afternoon. That way, you have time to eat lunch and maybe take a siesta. You will really enjoy the experience and not become stressed or over-drink by trying to hit too many tasting rooms in one day.

f. **Spit or Swallow?** – In my years working in tasting rooms, I remember just a few people spitting. Probably 90% of people who visit tasting rooms swallow the wine. Spitting is very important when you are evaluating a wine. As Jancis Robinson suggests, "spit with pride." This technique will help you to sensitize your palate, and will help you to unveil the truth of a wine. Be patient, however, because this takes time and practice.

g. **Be Polite** - Tasting rooms are not sports bars. Tasting rooms want to offer a sensorial experience with their wines, so it is very important to be conscious and polite with the employees and other patrons. Do not expect to drink all you want and being loud to the level that is obnoxious.

h. **Should We Bring the Kids?!** – If you bring kids, bring snacks, coloring books, or perhaps a tablet to keep them entertained. Although some tasting rooms welcome children more than others, it is always a better decision to take the afternoon/evening with your partner, friends, or family, as tasting rooms can become busy, loud and boring for kids, which can become stressful for the parents/caretakers.

i. **Should We Bring the Dog?!** – Not all tasting rooms allow animals, but if you are in Monterey, Carmel-by-the-Sea or Carmel Valley, these communities in general are very dog-friendly. As to other wine regions in California, I recommend you call ahead and ask.

Enhancing Our Appreciation of Wine and Food

Hippocrates
"Our food should be our medicine and our medicine should be our food."

"We should eat not only to survive but to flourish and enhance ourselves."

David M. Kaplan

Building an Appreciation for Food and Wine

Growing up in Chile, I automatically think of wine as food. I grew up in the south central part of Chile in Los Angeles (yes, there is another L.A. besides the one in California). A little about L.A. de Chile: With a population of around 185,000 people, Los Angeles is the capital of the Bío-Bío province in the VIII Region of the country. For many of you, the name "Bío-Bío" might sounds a little weird ... but Bío-Bío is a river and the name has a native Mapuche origin. It means "Big River" due to the fact that this river is the second largest river in Chile, more than 380 kilometers in length. This river was the frontier between the Spaniards and the Mapuches. For more than 300 years, the Spaniards were in war with the Mapuches, but they never conquered the southernmost areas of South America. This long relationship with the Spaniards evolved in assimilation and exchange from both sides, with diverse cultural influences like the development of local wine call *"chicha,"* perhaps the introduction and assimilation of the modern wine culture in Chile, and an amazing Spanish/Mapuche fusion cuisine call cocina criolla.

Chicha:
In Chile, the term refers to a beverage obtained by the partial fermentation of grape must.
Cocina Criolla:
is the gastronomical fusion of the Native and Spanish cuisine.

In terms of wine, the Bío-Bío region is becoming better known because of the excellent quality Pinot Noirs and Chardonnays coming from the area. Growing up in L.A. (Chile), I was fortunate because my father was excellent in the kitchen, as well as my mother, plus my father had extensive experience in the hospitality industry. He worked in Santiago as a waiter, bartender and cook a large portion of his life until he eventually settled in L.A. He then went on to become the concessionaire of the prestigious Club de la Union, way back in the 1970s. During that time I was a baby, so I have no recollection of this experience.

After the Club de la Union, my father got involved in the catering business for a short period of time and eventually, due to bad economic times in Chile, he was forced to change his job from culinary arts to the forestry industry, where he eventually retired. I have to say I feel lucky to have had the opportunity to enjoy my mother's and father's cooking, but I never thought about studying gastronomy ... instead, I became a social worker. I later realized food and wine are where my true passion lies and I feel this is a part of my DNA. Thank you, parents!

Fresh, seasonal food was very important for my family and in Los Angeles, it was readily available throughout the year due to the proximity to rural areas that always provided incredible varieties of fruits and vegetables, as well as fresh and diverse cheeses, meats and poultry. I hope that people down there will continue valuing and respecting their cultural treasure, even though today Chile is being invaded by corporations with the industrial food system model, causing major health issues like obesity.

The Money Factor

During my first years in the U.S., I was astonished by the number of fast-food eateries I encountered. It didn't take long to realize the strong disconnect from food that exists here, which lends itself to the lack of understanding of how important food is. I also realized there is a strong opinion among many in the U.S. that making food at home is costly and time consuming. Many of my first friends recommended that I eat in restaurants instead of cooking at home because it would be "cheaper."

After a decade in the country, I now know their rationale has its origin in the so-called "convenience factor." I have to admit that sometimes I have been trapped by the "convenience factor," but I still believe that with a little effort and desire, we can start cooking at home again.

Connecting with the Source

To be connected and educated about the source of food is critical in order to build an appreciation for it. Educational programs in our schools are a key factor to building an understanding at an early age about the origin and importance of food in our lives. Educational programs also develop respect for the people who grow our food, and an understanding of the fundamental role of Mother Nature in this beautiful process. We need to thank people like Alice Waters, Michael Pollan and so many others for bringing enlightenment to the subject, and also for being activists and strong promoters of different food programs for schools and universities in California and around the nation.

Though these programs created for schools and universities are wonderful, we cannot relegate that responsibility solely to formal educational institutions ... as with all things, the parental influence and role is fundamental in the quest to recover the rituals of eating. Whether eating at the table or bringing more awareness to food, family influence is essential.

I excerpted a couple of paragraphs from the book *Cooked* by Michael Pollan, because I think these two paragraphs encapsulate the importance of recovering the table rituals:

"So it will come as no surprise that the decline in home cooking closely tracks the rise in obesity and all the chronic diseases linked to diet. The rise of fast food and the decline in home cooking have also undermined the institution of the shared meal by encouraging us to eat different things and to eat on the run and often alone." –Michael Pollan

"It is a foundation of family life, the place where our children learn the art of conversation and acquire the habits of civilization: Sharing, listening, taking turns, navigating differences, arguing without offending." –Michael Pollan

Educating ourselves is very important and in many cases more important than money. I did not grow up in a wealthy family, and certainly after my dad lost his job at the Club de la Union, financial struggles continued to deepen for my family. Regardless of our financial status, something my parents always valued and gave their children was the value/appreciation for food and wine, wine as an extension of the meal. I have a son and as a father one of my goals is to transfer the same appreciation for food and wine ... besides transferring my sense of humor, of course!

Wine & Food Pairing

Wine and food pairing is something that everybody does in an unconscious way. One of the best ways to understand wine and food pairing is through exploring the local cuisine of particular wine producing regions, the foods the residents enjoy and pair with their wines. I completely believe that a big part of the culture of an individual is encapsulated in the food and beverage the person consumes. Here in the U.S., people pair muffins with milk, or fries with a soda, to cleanse the palate. This is a very basic example of beverage and food pairing, though no less important. Now we can take the same example and be fancier about it, so the same chocolate muffin can be paired with a port and the fries with a glass of Champagne or sparkling wine … I think you get the idea. Is my hope that this section will facilitate the understanding of how to pair wine with food, and vice-versa. It is important to explore different options so you can guide yourself in the world of wine and food pairing. My suggestion is to always be open to explore different options. It is my hope that exploring options will bring more pleasure in to your life.

What do you need to know when you're planning on pairing a dish with wine?

There are a few fundamental techniques that can be used to pair a dish with wine, along with a sense of creative exploration. Practice! Meaning, start cooking again. Know your food, where and how it's grown. If you don't know how to cook, take a class or get together with friends who know how to do it or have the intention to learn, and together the group can practice at home. Cooking is fun and an excellent opportunity to gather with others, making it a social event, or perhaps an event to entertain your kids if you invite them to be participants. The cooking process is fun for them and is a learning experience at the same time. I enjoy involving my son as much as I can in the kitchen and I already see some very good results because of that.

Practice is the number one method in any technique to see improvement, and for the most part, you can't go wrong when you are pairing wine and food … however, the goal for this section is to learn how to satisfy the intrinsic, hedonistic aspect of any human being, which is pleasuring our senses. Outlined below is a framework of steps to help guide you on your food and wine pairing journey. I hope using these techniques will help you reach ultimate pleasure for your senses!

First Step: Planning. Base ingredients need to be selected and are fundamental, so be sure your base ingredients are of good quality. Buy your produce in a farmers market and, if it is possible, organically grown or as little pesticide use as possible, if you cannot get organic. In the case of poultry and red meats, be sure the animals are grass fed. I know some of you may be thinking, "yes, but that is much more expensive." I invite you to change your mentality about that because when you feed yourself, it is OK to spend a little more because you are taking care of your body. Quality, nutritious and delicious food for you and your family … don't you think you deserve that?! At the same time, you are supporting farmers who are conscientious and care about their animals and the environment. Very importantly, they care about you. If you grow your own food, even better! The more we know about the origin of our food, the better.

Let's identify the most common base ingredients:

• Meat, poultry, game, shellfish, seafood, legumes, vegetables, and fruits.

Second Step: Know what cooking method or technique to apply to the base ingredients. Every option from now on will begin narrowing the selection of your wine.

What are the most common cooking methods?

• Steaming and Poaching
• Sautéing
• Braise & Stewing
• Pan-Searing and Roasting
• Grilling
• Barbecuing
• Deep Frying

Descriptions of cooking methods:

I. Steaming and Poaching

• **Steaming** is a moist-heat cooking technique that employs hot steam to conduct the heat to the base ingredient that you are planning to cook. Once water is heated past the 212°F mark, it turns into steam. When you apply a steaming technique, there is no agitation involved, so it is gentler on delicate base ingredients like fruits, vegetables and seafood. Steam produces the most "subtle and delicate flavors," and because of that, this technique is most commonly paired with delicate wines. Some delicate wines are dry white and Rosés, wines with little or no oak. In the case of reds, the ones that by essence are delicate include Beaujolais, Pinot Noir, and Rioja Tempranillos, to name a few.

• **Poaching** means to cook something in liquid with a temperature ranging from 140°F to 180°F. Poaching is typically a delicate cooking technique that is applied to very delicate items like eggs, vegetables and fish. Other meat options like chicken are often prepared via poaching, too. If you would like to add more body to the dish, poaching in butter or olive oil can lend a rich bridge to Chardonnay with some medium oak character. Poaching with butter or olive oil can also lend an interesting contrast to wines with substantial acidity like sparkling wines, Cava, Prosseco or Champagne, also whites like Chablis, Sauvignon Blanc, Pinot Gris, Sauvignon Gris, etc.

II. Sautéing
Is basically a dry-heat cooking technique. In order to apply this technique more effectively you need to add a little butter, oil, or animal fat to a very hot pan to cook the food very quickly. Sautéing will brown the food's surface as it cooks and it will develop complex flavors and aromas.

   *If you want to add richness and more body, use butter, oil, or animal fats

   *Caramelization builds a bridge to oaky wines, whites, and reds.

   * Pan sauces provide opportunities to integrate acids, fats, wine, herbs and other bridge ingredients that create complex flavors.

III. Braising and Stewing
• **Braising** is a form of moist-heat cooking that breaks down connective tissues in tough cuts of meat, leaving them tender and succulent. Braising and stewing often are techniques that create the most intense flavors.

   *When you braise or stew, meat flavors tend to be very well integrated from long, slow cooking.

*Stock and wine-base reductions liquids can be very full-bodied and intense, especially if reduced substantially. In that case we need to use wines that counterbalance the richness. Some examples are: Syrah, Grenache, Carmenere, Zinfandel, Malbec, Cabernet Sauvignon, Petit Verdot, Barolos, Barbarescos and Blens.

IV. Pan-Searing and Roasting

Are among the best and most efficient cooking methods around. Pan roasting takes advantage of conductive heat from the stove plus radiant and convective heat in the oven to cook thicker cuts of meat perfectly and in a short amount of time. With pan-searing, you can create deep caramelization which creates a solid bridge to medium and full-body wines. The protein in rare to medium meats neutralize tannins, and fats baste the meat during cooking. This adds body and richness, and reduces the impression of bitterness and/or tannins in wine. So in terms of wine, you can use wines that are high in tannins like Barolos, Barbarescos, Cabernet Sauvignon, Petit Syrah, Syrah, Tannat, Zinfandel and Blens.

V. Broiling and Grilling

Are not too different. Grilling involves heating the food from below, while broiling involves heating from above. Both are done at high temperatures (over 300 degrees). Regarding grilling or broiling, you sear what you are cooking to keep the juices sealed in. That is why this method needs to be done at very high temperature. In both cases, the food is typically turned once during cooking and a grid or grate of some kind is used. This gives food the distinctive grill marks that are the hallmark of this cooking technique. I will suggest mid to full-body reds and blends to pair with grilling dishes, also Rosés and Champagne.

*Rubs, marinades, and condiments provide a simple and direct means for incorporating bridge flavors.

VI. Barbecuing

Is often used in the same verbal context as the term grilling, but they are very different. I grew up in a place where barbeque was a deep part of the culture; every weekend, Chileans engage in barbeques with friends and family. This is one aspect of Chile I deeply miss! After I moved to the U.S., I almost became a vegetarian when I learned about factory farming, which was a foreign concept to me in Chile. (I am unsure how things are now, but during my time in Chile, factory farming was not a common practice.) Part of the reason I considered reducing my consumption of meat is because grass-fed livestock is not largely available, it is more costly, and over time I learned more about the health benefits of consuming less meat, as well as the negative repercussions industrialized farming has on the environment. Now consuming meat and barbecuing has become a special occasion type of thing. If you have the chance to visit South America, in particular Chile, Argentina, or Uruguay, you'll find the best barbeques ever with clean meats from animals that were well taken care of. My recommendation is probably a little biased because I haven't been to Texas or the southern U.S. yet, and I hear those regions are well known for barbeque. Getting back to barbecuing ... traditionally, cooking is done slowly with low temperatures and a lot of smoke. Whether you are barbecuing vegetables, chicken, lamb or beef, wines to consider can vary from Rosé, Champagne or sparkling wines, to Tempranillos, Merlot, Barbera, Sangiovese, Cabernet Franc, Cabernet Sauvignon, Carménère, Syrah and Blens.

VII. Deep Frying

Involves submerging food in hot, liquid fat/oil. Surprisingly, this is actually a form of dry-heat cooking. The use of proper temperature in deep-frying is fundamental and requires always keeping the oil at temperatures between 325°F and 400°F. Hotter than that and the oil may start to smoke. If it's any cooler, it starts to seep into the food and make it greasy. This technique creates the classic crunchy texture a lot of us enjoy. Food cooked using this type of technique is best paired with wines that are light, crisp, with nice acidity, and why not add some fun with bubbles (Champagne or sparkling wine. For example, any white wine with oak, dry Rosés, light young reds with little to no oak, or delicious sparkling wines.

Third Step: Bridge ingredients. These ingredients will continue to narrow down the options for wine selection with your final meal. Let's see some of them and their function!

Bridge Ingredients

Bridge ingredients, as the name literally describes, create a bridge between your base ingredient and the wine that you would like to pair the meal with. The bridge ingredients help connect base ingredients to varietal wines through their own acidity, body and flavors.

To give you an idea: when you use heavy bridge ingredients like reductions, sauces, fats, cheeses and strong herbs, these add body and richness to the base ingredients, but they also add very important flavors that will help connect the dish with a full-body wine. As you can see, one main function of bridge ingredients is to add body, texture, viscosity and flavor to the dish. Bridge ingredients can be simple or complex, subtle or powerful.

Some common bridge ingredients:
- Oils and Fats
- Spices
- Herbs-Fresh and Dried
- Vegetables
- Mushrooms
- Fruits Fresh and Dried
- Dairy and Cheeses
- Cured and Smoked Meats
- Nuts
- Wine, Beer and Spirits

Fats and Oils are some of the most commonly used bridge ingredients. They help reduce the impression of bitterness and astringency in wines and add fatty richness or "body" to the dish. These are good bridge ingredients to complement with buttery wines such as (some) Chardonnays.

Remember, when pairing wine with food, you need to consider the cooking method, texture, temperature, environmental factors and the company. All these elements are very important! Every base and bridge ingredient has its own acidity, texture, body and flavors just like the wines do.

Body

Wine professionals, sommeliers and chefs/cooks always talk about the body and texture of food. The "body" of food (and wine) refers to weight or fullness on the palate. Similar body styles in wine and food generally work well together. For example, a Cabernet Sauvignon (full body wine) pairs well with a grilled rib-eye steak, (a full body food). In contrast, dissimilar body styles often leave one element in the dust like pairing that same Cabernet with a steamed chicken dish (a delicate body food with a full body wine). There certainly are exceptions to the rule, such as pairing a Cabernet with barbecued chicken. This works well because barbecuing the chicken give a full body character and texture to the chicken. Taking it further, adding some smoky sauce, such as barbecue sauce, will bridge the wine and food even better.

What is the function of the BODY? We always hear about "body" in wine and when I started exploring the world of wine, I thought, "How sexy it is to describe a beverage using the analogy of the body!" For instance, I was imagining conversations with my friends, analyzing wine legs and saying, "Hey guys, look at this wine, it is very voluptuous like Pamela Anderson," or maybe, "This one is very thin like Mick Jagger!" In any case, it became easy for me to observe legs (perhaps I was already good at observing legs ...). Wine became more interesting when I discovered that I was able to figure out the viscosity and the alcohol level, just from observing and analyzing legs. How cool is that! Body also has a lot to do in how we pair wine with food, so after all it is very important to pay attention to those qualities.

Components of wine body:
- Flavor Concentration
- Viscosity, Alcohol
- Fruit Structure
- Acidity
- Oak
- Tannin, (texture, astringency)

Components of food body:
- Flavor Concentration
- Fat (richness)
- Seasoning/Spices
- Texture
- Cooking Technique

Herbs

One of my own projects is to create an herb garden. Imagine making pizzas, and/or salads (among the many dishes that require herbs) ... wouldn't it be awesome to walk a few steps to your garden and select the proper herbs! Herbs play an important role in wine and food pairing as well. There are two main categories of herbs: Fine herbs (delicate) and strong herbs (resinous).

Most Common Fine Herbs:
- Parsley
- Chervil
- Chives
- Tarragon
- Dill
- Basil
- Bay leaves
- Cilantro

Most Common Strong Herbs:
- Thyme
- Mint
- Oregano
- Marjoram
- Sage
- Rosemary

Some of these strong herbs have a piney aroma and flavor that can pair well with full-bodied reds, wines with an earthy, rustic, and dry character. Think Greek, Italian, French, and Portuguese wines.

When it comes to white wines, it is important to use strong herbs in moderation. Strong herbs can overpower certain wines, but in moderation can be a very stable bridge ingredient. These may pair well with light to medium-bodied whites with nice acidity, for example, Pinot Grigio, Risling, Sauvignon Blanc, Chablis, and Champagne.

Complimentary and Contrasting Flavors

Chefs and/or cooks use different techniques in the kitchen, but certainly these two basic philosophies for pairing food and wine are one of the most important ones.

Complementary Flavors

• They make sense together ... like Dean Martin and Jerry Lewis.

• Create an effective bridge, such as similar levels of acidity and body styles. For example, a buttery dish pairs with a creamy Chardonnay.

• Do not imitate or mirror another completely, but are related. For example, The Three Stooges. They are kind of similar but different at the same time, right?! In terms of food, a good example will be pairing lobster with Chardonnay or pairing oysters or/and shellfish with Champagne, Chablis, Sauvignon Blanc, or perhaps any type of wine that is fairly acidic and lemony.

Contrasting Flavors

• Are fundamentally different. Think Don Quixote de la Mancha and Sancho Panza. Quixote was an idealist living in his own world and Sancho Panza was completely the opposite ... realistic and rational. Perhaps you can use your husband or wife in this analogy ... oops! Not good idea.

In food, fries and sparkling wine would be the example. Why? Fries are salty, crunchy and a little (or a lot) greasy. Champagne or sparkling wine, on the other hand, is for the most part crisp, refreshing, and has nice acidity that cleanses the palate. Champagne or sparkling wine also prepares your palate for another helping of fries. Here contrasting flavors work together to stimulate the palate, like acidity and saltines or lemon and salt.

• Contrasting flavors provide balance and interest, especially when food and wine have a strong base of complementary flavors to build on. It is like the yin and yang in Eastern philosophy.

Don't forget that food and wine flavor is determined by a number of different factors, including taste, smell, color, texture, temperature and overall appearance, as well as the physiological and psychological conditions of the plants and animals you will be eating.

As for pairing wine with food, in a dish we look for balance. A delicate yet important balancing act is the ultimate expression of gastronomic pleasure. Within that balance is a maximum expression or "climax" that the wine and food encompass together which creates the final act of pleasure. To help you reach that high level of gastronomic climax, I suggest balancing taste principles of food with various wines.

Food Sensations
I. Sweet Foods
II. Bitter Foods
III. Sour Foods
IV. Salty Foods
V. Umami Foods

I. Sweet Foods
Contrast: Pair dishes with sweet elements like salads, pad Thai, or Chinese chow mein with wines that have a hint or more of sweetness and with a fair amount of acidity like Voudre (Chenin Blanc) and Kabinet Rieslings.

Compliment: Pair desserts with wines as sweet as or sweeter than the dessert. It is common to pair desserts with wines like Sauternes, Tokay and late harvest Rieslings.

II. Bitter Foods
Contrast: To counterbalance bitter foods like barbeques, they should be paired with wines that have fruity characteristics.

Compliment: There are some common food elements that can add bitterness to a dish, such as coffee, olives, beer, citrus peel, horseradish, wild lettuce, roasted walnuts and almonds, to list a few. When used, some of these elements create a bridge to complement the dish with tannic (bitter) wines.

III. Sour Foods
Contrast: Pair sour foods with wines that are sweet or have a hint of sweetness. This contrast creates a nice balance between the wine and the dish. Chenin Blanc, Gewurztraminer, Moscato or Riesling can make the magic.

Complement: Complement dishes that are high in acidity with a wine containing a high level of acidity; this brings harmony and balance. For instance, think of oysters. If you add lemon juice to them and maybe a little hot sauce, in order to complement this dish you need a wine with a fair amount of acidity and lemony character as well. Same with ceviche. Remember, ceviche is traditionally made with raw fish and flavored using lemon juice. In that case, think of wines that contain a fair amount of acidity and crispiness like Brut sparkling wines, Cava, Prosseco or Champagnes, Sauvignon Blanc (Sancerre), Pinot Blanc, Vinho Verde, Verdejo etc.

IV. Salty Foods
Sometimes foods are naturally salty (caviar), while others are salty because salt has been added (fries). Either way, contrast is always the way to go.

Contrast: Counterbalance salty foods with acidic wines like Vihno Verde, Brut sparkling wines, Sauvignon Blanc, to mention a few, or semi-sweet (off-dry) wines such as Chenin Blanc or Kabinet Riesling, for example.

V. Umami
Until the 1990s, umami wasn't known in Western cuisine, at least, not under this name. It has been commonly used among chefs and in kitchens for a long time, but until the discovery of umami, we didn't know much about it. Umami has been part of Western cuisine for a long time, with many foods and dishes that contain umami. It is very important to consider because in my experience, foods that have a strong umami presence, like sushi or smoked salmon, require wines with a low level of tannins. White, dry Rosés and sparkling wines are good examples. Tannic red wines such as Cabernet Sauvignon, Tannat, Barolos, Barbarbescos, and Shiraz usually leave a metallic aftertaste.

More about Umami:
• Discovered by Japanese scientist Kikunae Ikeda in the late 1980s.

• Umami is also known as Monosodium Glutamate (MSG). It is considered a new seasoning in the West but has been around for centuries in Eastern cultures.

• The flavor is described as savory or delicious.

In what food do you find umami?
Usually you'll find umami in meats, poultry, seafood, vegetables, cheeses and sauces, such as soy sauce, fish sauce and ketchup. Umami is also found in cured meats such as smoked or natural ham, bacon, sausage, pepperoni, salami, Serrano ham and prosciutto. Seafood such as dried and cured fish and shellfish (predominantly) also contain umami. You may also find umami in dairy products.

The following are some examples of cheeses that contain umami:

- Parmesan
- Romano
- Swiss Emmental
- Gruyere
- Cheddar
- Roquefort
- Blue Cheese
- Pretty much any aged cheese

The following are some examples of vegetables that contain umami:

- Tomatoes, dried or fresh
- Tomatoes sauce
- Ketchup
- Asparagus
- Spinach
- Celery
- Cabbage
- Green peas
- Onion
- Mushrooms

Closing Remarks

My wish is that this book contributes to your journey of wine and food appreciation, and also encourages you to build an understanding of the intrinsic value of purchasing and consuming quality, nutritious food and wine. It is important to support farmers markets as well as organic and non-GMO products, when possible, in order to support producers who have integrity and make a product that is good for your family, animals and the environment. As my parents always told me, when you cook, don't forget the most important, yet intangible, ingredient in the kitchen, which is "Cariño." In Chile, "cariño" means love and trust me, when you make food with your cariño, it is always delicious!

Food

Once upon a time,

Human beings understood the sound of the elements.

As humans we knew how to dance the beautiful melody of the seasons.

We understood we were part of the whole and the whole was part of us, as the fish in the ocean and the worm in the soil.

Today we are disconnected with the source of our existence.

Beyond spirituality we lose respect for ourselves and our environment.

It is time to recover and re-discover the rituals and ceremonies of sharing and enjoying a meal at the table with family and friends.

It is time to understand that food is not a simple vehicle to satisfy the basic need of hunger.

Food is an intimate communion between the universe and us.

Pablo Antinao

Acknowledgments

I would like to express my profound gratitude to the people who contributed to this book:

Amparo Phillips, for her beautiful work of illustrations and graphic design of T A S T E.

Patricia Hamilton, for the publication and guidance of this work.

Joyce Krieg, for the preliminary editing of this work.

Karla Maribel Orellana, for the final editing of this work.

Kelley Williams, for my profile picture.

The Burnison family for all the constant support I will always be deeply grateful.

The Pagoulatos family, for the support and dedication in taking care of the more precious gift of my life, my son Dimitri.

My son Dimitri, who brought the pleasure and honor to be a father and the inspiration for this book.

I would especially like to thank Elizabeth Burnison for all her support for this book and for her dedication to the pre-editing process.

Salud!

Resources

Johnson, Hugh. The World Atlas of Wine. New York: Simon & Schuster fourth edition, 1998.

Julyan, Brian. Sales and service for the wine professional. London: South- Western Third Edition, 2008.

Lenoir, Jean. Le Nez Du Vin. Editions Jean Lenoir, 2006.

Lenoir, Jean. Wine Faults Le Nez Du Vin. Editions Jean Lenoir, 2006.

Stevenson, Tom. Sotheby's World Wine Encyclopedia. London and New York: Dorling Kindersley publishers, 2005.

Waterhouse, Andrew. Introduction to winemaking. Department of Viticulture and Enology University of California Davis, California. 2006.

Thomas Pinney. A History of Wine in America; From the beginning to Prohibition Volume I and II, University of California Press, Berkeley, Los Angeles and London, 1989.

Catena Laura, Vino Argentino: An Insider's Guide to The Wines and Wine Country of Argentina. Chronicle Books LLC, 2010.

Alvarado Rodrigo. Chilean Wine. The Heritage. The Wine Appreciation Guild, 2005.

Goode Jamie, The Science of Wine: From Vine to Glass, University of California Press, Berkeley and Los Angeles, Second edition 2014.

Goleman Daniel, Focus: The Hidden Driver of Excellence. Library of Congress Cataloging-in-Publication Data. 2013.

Pollan Michael, Omnivore's Dilema: A Natural History Of Four Meals. The Penguin Group, 2006.

Pollan Michael, Cooked: A Natural History of Transformation. The Penguin Press, New York, 2013.

Tannahill Reay, Food in History. Three Rivers Press. New York. 1988, 1973.

Bonné Jon, The New California Wine: A guide to the Producers and Wines Behind a Revolution in Taste. Ten Speed Press, Berkeley California, 2014.

Asimov Eric, How to Love Wine: A memoir and Manifesto. Library of Congress Cataloging-in-Publication Data. 2012.

Maturana R. Humberto. La Objetividad: Un argumento Para Obligar. Dolmes Ediciones S.A., 1997.

Robinson Jancis, Harding Julia and Vouillamoz . Wine Grapes: A Complete Guide to 1.368 Vine Varieties, including their origin and flavors. Harper Collins Publishers. 2012.

Fielden Christopher. Exploring The World Of Wines and Spirits. Wine and Spirit Education Trust. 2009, 2010.

Robinson, Jancis, Murphy Linda, American Wine: The Ultimate Companion to the Wines and Wineries of the United States. University California Press, Berkeley and Los Angeles, California. 2013.

David M. Kaplan, The Philosophy of Food. University of California Press, Berkeley and Los Angeles. California 2012.

Alcohol and Tax Trade Bureau, U.S. Department of Treasury, http://www.ttb.gov

United States Department of Agriculture, http://www.usda.gov/wps/portal/usda/usdahome?navid=organic-agriculture

The Wine Institute, http://www.wineinstitute.org

Pablo Antinao is a certified wine professional from the Culinary Institute of America (CIA) and certified sommelier from the Academy of Sommeliers in Barcelona, Spain.
Pablo is the founder of *Bakai Wine + Tapas* in Monterey California and conducts wine workshops throughout Silicon Valley and the Monterey Peninsula.
A native from Los Angeles, Chile, Pablo resides in California.

GOOD TASTE

GOOD **TASTE**

www.ingramcontent.com/pod-product-compliance
Lightning Source LLC
Chambersburg PA
CBHW050755110526
44538CB00002B/12